D0367985

# WRITING WORLD WAR II

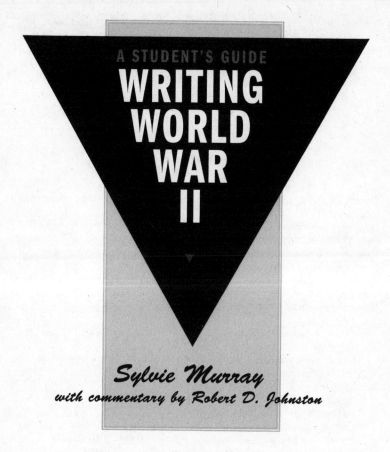

A STUDENT'S GUIDE

# WRITING WORLD WAR II

*Sylvie Murray*

*with commentary by Robert D. Johnston*

**HILL AND WANG**

*A division of Farrar, Straus and Giroux   New York*

Hill and Wang
A division of Farrar, Straus and Giroux
18 West 18th Street, New York 10011

Copyright © 2011 by Sylvie Murray
Commentator's note, commentary, and afterword copyright © 2011
by Robert D. Johnston
All rights reserved
Distributed in Canada by D&M Publishers, Inc.
Printed in the United States of America
First edition, 2011

Grateful acknowledgment is made for permission to reprint the following previously published material:
"Writing Home: Intimate Conversations About War," from the *Journal of Historical Biography* 6 (Autumn 2009). Reprinted with permission.
Illustrations on pages 65 (bottom) and 69 courtesy of the Hennepin County Library, Kittleson World War II Collection.
Illustrations on pages 60, 62, 63, and 65 (top) courtesy of the University of North Texas Digital Library.
Illustration on page 67 courtesy of the Library of Congress.

Library of Congress Cataloging-in-Publication Data
Murray, Sylvie.
    Writing World War II : a student's guide / Sylvie Murray ; with commentary by
Robert D. Johnston. — 1st ed.
        p.   cm.
    Includes bibliographical references and index.
    ISBN 978-0-8090-8549-1 (pbk. : alk. paper)
    1. World War, 1939–1945—United States—Historiography.   2. World War,
1939–1945—Social aspects—United States—Historiography.   3. Nationalism—
United States—History—20th century—Historiography.   4. Political culture—United
States—History—20th century—Historiography.   5. Citizenship—United States—
History—20th century—Historiography.   6. United States—Social conditions—
1933–1945—Historiography.   7. United States—Politics and government—
1933–1945—Historiography.   8. Historiography—Study and teaching—United
States.   I. Johnston, Robert D.   II. Title.   III. Title: Writing World War 2.   IV. Title:
Writing World War Two.

D769.1.M875 2010
940.53'73072—dc22

                                                                          2011000860

Designed by Abby Kagan

www.fsgbooks.com

1   3   5   7   9   10   8   6   4   2

*For Michelle, Christopher, and Alexa*

# CONTENTS

# CONTENTS

# PREFACE

The main purpose of *Writing World War II* is to invite students to think critically about historical writing itself. The choices historians make—conscious or not, explicit or not—shape the historical narratives they present. Historians select particular primary and secondary sources, they decide which events and actors will be given prominence in the stories they tell, and they derive meaning from the material they choose to examine. The art of interpretation is at the heart of the historian's craft. Through a series of essays on the American experience of World War II and short commentaries that point to the interpretive choices that underpin these essays, this book seeks to elucidate for students these basic principles of historical writing.

The volume's core consists of nine historical essays, divided into three parts. Each essay examines one aspect of changing and contested definitions of national identity. Questions pertaining to the nationalist or internationalist nature of American identity, to the political culture of America at war, and to citizens' experiences of war are explored. The short introduction and the commentary that frame each part of the book are intended to illustrate the historical method. While the introduction will alert the reader to some of the choices made by the author, a critique offered by the historian Robert D. Johnston at the end of each part will dissect the author's interpretive and narrative strategies.

Our narrative opens, in part I, on the period prior to the attack on Pearl Harbor and to America's entrance in the world war as a belligerent. Here we ask readers to cast aside a widely held postwar conviction that the war had to be fought, in order to immerse themselves in a time when Americans were bitterly divided over whether they should go to war. President Roosevelt's insistence that the nation's security was at stake in the global conflict, the debates over intervention that bitterly divided Americans before December 1941, and the marginal place attributed to these debates in the paradigm of "the Good War" constitute the focus of our examination here. These essays highlight the strong nationalist and realist accents of American political culture in the pre–Pearl Harbor era. Bluntly put, America did not join the war out of a sense of responsibility to the free world.

Part II examines the political culture of America at war. Focusing first on the material produced by the promoters of America's war effort, one is struck by the multiplicity, even the inconsistency, of the rhetorical strategies used to "create a will to win." Values that may appear at first sight contradictory—individualism and collective purpose, diversity and unity—were reconciled in ways that were at times more creative than credible. The posters crafted to support mobilization, for instance, offer historians a rich, and complex, visual landscape. This body of sources, a scholarly commentary on it, and a topical essay reveal the multiple traditions at work in wartime political culture and the gendered dimensions of that call to service.

In part III, the words of propagandists are replaced with those of ordinary Americans. Did the various experiences of war cement a common bond among American citizens, or did they reinforce the divisions that already existed within the American nation? Did they draw new boundaries of inclusion in, and exclusion from, the benefits and duties of citizenship? Americans experienced not one but several different wars; this is especially true of combat troops, conscientious objectors, and cultural and racial minorities. Although many aspects of Americans' wartime experiences strengthened the ties of national citizenship—or so it appeared after the fact—during the war itself, tangible tensions troubled Americans.

Readers will have noticed by now that they will not find in this book a comprehensive history of World War II, either in its global dimensions or in the multiple ways this tremendous moment in recent history affected American society in particular. The military and diplomatic aspects of the war have been left out, as have other topics that, some may argue, should be included in any book about World War II. As the commentator has pointed out in his closing remarks, it may appear astounding that the use of the atomic bomb, to name only one of the most glaring omissions, has found no room in this volume. Clusters of books on several other important subjects are sitting on my shelf, unused. I have mentioned in the book's conclusion some of the topics that I would have liked to delve into had I had the time and space to do so; there are others. At several stages in the process of writing this book I had to remind myself that complete coverage was not the intended purpose. In the end, what I hope to have achieved through this series of essays is a text that engages students and teachers of history in a dialogue about the stories we tell about the past, and the ways in which we tell them.

# COMMENTATOR'S NOTE
## by *Robert D. Johnston*

This is an unusual book, if only because I am not the author but will be commenting on the author's work within these pages. The goal of my commentary is to further the work that Sylvie Murray has already done so well in the main body of the book—and that is, in her words, to demonstrate "the critical role that interpretive choices play in the writing of history."

The idea that interpretive choices are central to historical thinking and writing necessarily implies *pluralism*. Unfortunately, far too much historical writing occurs as if there were one—and only one—story. Textbooks almost always commit the sin of telling a singular historical story, using an authoritative, monolithic voice to provide the One True Account that students need to know. Yet impressive works of historical scholarship also far too often use a godlike narrative to establish an argument that the author clearly feels can't be argued with.

Such omniscience violates some of the most fundamental canons of historical thought. As the cantankerous historical educator James Loewen eloquently argues, "history is furious debate informed by reason and evidence."[1]

And debate implies that there is more than one legitimate perspective, interpretation, argument, set of sources, and way of narrating stories. To be sure, there are facts, and there is truth. But beyond some of the basics (e.g., the United States declared war on Japan on December 8, 1941), we as readers of history place ourselves in the hands of authors who actively choose which questions to raise, which sources to emphasize, which ethical lessons to pass on, and which stories to tell.

One of Sylvie Murray's most important achievements in this book is that she makes her choices uncommonly transparent. To be sure, hers is an extremely insightful and well-argued book that helps advance our thinking about World War II. But even more fundamentally, Murray celebrates the idea of historical pluralism. Let a thousand historians' voices, and a thousand historians' interpretations, flower!

That is also where my commentary comes in. I, too, celebrate a multitude of voices and interpretations. My job is to help you as students to continue reflecting, in an even more sustained manner, on the choices that Murray has made. At times I will do this by largely agreeing with her, in those cases in which she has truly won me over with the originality of her thinking and the power of her arguments. Other times, when I think she has interpreted an issue in a way that just doesn't make as much intellectual sense as it might, I will disagree. And sometimes I will simply point out other roads not taken.

The ultimate goal, then, will be for you to join us with your own commentaries, your own interpretations, your own insights. Any good reading of historical scholarship begins with active questioning, a critical mind-set, and a commitment to make up your mind about the big issues at play. That's what we invite you to bring to this project.

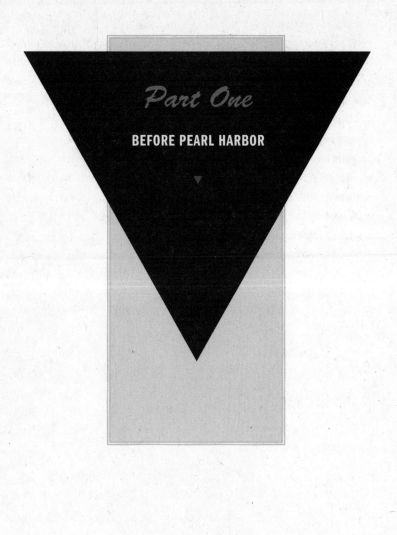

# Part One

## BEFORE PEARL HARBOR

▼

The period of nonbelligerency from 1939 to 1941 is often considered marginal to the more important story of America at war—a mere prelude to the full-scale mobilization in the defense of freedom that followed the United States' entrance into World War II. But the reluctance on the part of the United States to get involved in the European war that had begun in September 1939 deserves sustained attention. The following three essays employ three distinct modes of historical writing to examine the highly nationalist and realist tone of American political debates in the pre–Pearl Harbor era.

The first essay examines, through a close reading of primary documents, the emphasis on national security that dominated public debates and policies in that period. While the historical argument presented here is not original, using primary sources allows one to appreciate the decidedly marginal role that democratic and humanitarian principles occupied in that story, with tragic consequences for the world. Thus, a set of public speeches delivered by President Franklin Delano Roosevelt as the war unfolded in Europe forms the focus of inquiry. Roosevelt's words and his relative silence on the fate of European Jews then facing murderous violence are set in the context of congressional reluctance to intervene in the European war or to open the nation's door to refugees.

The second essay analyzes textbook narratives to examine how the debate about intervention is presented to undergraduate students. The reasons for opposing the European fight against fascism were varied, some more legitimate than others. But regardless of their merit, we err when we discredit anti-interventionism by associating it with narrow "isolationism" or reducing it to antisemitism, as some of the textbook accounts do. The textbook review is not commonly used in undergraduate composition, even though it has become an acknowledged mode of historiographical writing in the profession.[1] It can also be a difficult exercise to engage in because of the muted interpretive voice in which most textbooks are written. Yet dissecting and comparing textbook narratives— even just a few—can be a valuable tool for students to hone their critical reading and writing skills.

The short final essay presents a review of the paradigm of the Good War, explaining the use of that phrase by the journalist Tom Brokaw and the historian Stephen Ambrose, who have popularized it, and situating their interpretation against contrasting narratives. Because the topic carries widespread interest beyond scholarly circles, the work of nonhistorians is included. Even though the essay focuses on my own criticism of the work reviewed, its purpose is not to take a position forcefully in favor of or against the paradigm. This format is particularly useful in the case of a complex and highly polarized debate, in which the writer might want to reflect on the positions taken by different authors rather than try to persuade readers.

## IN THE NAME OF NATIONAL SECURITY

Franklin D. Roosevelt was a committed internationalist and a humanitarian, but he was also a realist, a pragmatist, who knew full well the limitations imposed by congressional and public opinion. His abiding faith in Christian and humanitarian ideals was expressed, for instance, in his annual message to Congress on January 4, 1939: "There comes a time in the affairs of men when they must prepare to defend, not their homes alone, but the tenets of faith and humanity on which their churches, their governments and their very civilization are founded." Two years later, as he was about to embark on his fight for congressional approval of the Lend-Lease bill, he offered in a stirring speech to Congress the memorable vision of "a world founded upon four essential human freedoms"—the freedom of speech and expression, the freedom to worship, the freedom from want, and the freedom from fear— that he pledged to secure "everywhere in the world." But these idealistic calls for action, along with the humanitarian ideals that motivated them and the commitment to international responsibility that they required, took a backseat prior to U.S. involvement. As noted by the historian Lawrence Levine, in the Four Freedoms speech, the president "was clearly endeavoring to supplement the

nation's practical need for security against Axis aggression—
which thus far had been his emphasis—with a vision of the kind
of world 'attainable in our own time and generation.' It was still
another attempt to persuade the American people to see the current wars in Europe and Asia in larger perspective." The "nar-
rower" perspective that dominated the pre–Pearl Harbor period
was more pragmatic than idealistic. As summarized by the historian Michael Sherry, "Throughout 1940, Roosevelt stressed the
nature of modern warfare more than the evil of fascism or the
virtue of nations resisting it. Issuing little uplifting Wilsonian rhetoric, he instead offered a drumbeat about the cold realities of the
world."[1] In Roosevelt's public addresses, as in the country's response
to the atrocities committed by the fascist and militarist regimes
abroad, national security and the national interest occupied center stage.

Cognizant of the strong congressional determination to avoid
multilateral entanglements, the president steered a cautious course
on international matters. The Senate's refusal in 1919 to join the
League of Nations—the centerpiece of Woodrow Wilson's idealistic vision of international cooperation—set the tone for the independent foreign policy carried out by the United States in the
1920s and 1930s. During Roosevelt's first term in office, Congress
reasserted its intention not to get dragged into another European
war. In 1930, the award-winning film *All Quiet on the Western Front*
(based on the novel written by a German veteran, Erich Maria
Remarque) had vividly recalled the brutality and senselessness of
the Great War of 1914–1918. The 1934 bestselling exposé *Merchants
of Death*, and sensationalized congressional hearings chaired by
the North Dakota senator Gerald Nye in 1934–1936, had drawn
attention to the role of profiteering bankers and munitions makers
in drawing the United States into the conflict. Mistrust for multilateral commitments was fed by the inability of European countries,
in the midst of the economic recession, to pay their World War I

debts. As a result, Congress passed in 1934 the Johnson Debt Default Act, which prohibited the extension of private or public loans to countries in default on their debt payments. The Neutrality Laws adopted in the second half of the 1930s—which banned the sale of arms (1935) and the extension of loans (1936) to nations at war, and required belligerents trading with the United States to pay cash for the goods they purchased and to transport them on non-U.S. ships (1937)—imposed significant restrictions on the nation's ability to intervene, indirectly, in international conflicts. Hence, as tensions abroad mounted, and as Congress was determined to avoid repeating the "mistakes" of World War I, the president found himself on the defensive and incapable of exercising the strong leadership on which he had thrived in his first years in office.[2]

In March 1938, Germany annexed Austria; in October it occupied western Czechoslovakia, followed by the rest of that country in March 1939; and it invaded Poland on September 1, 1939. After France and Britain declared war on Germany two days later, Roosevelt sought to build up America's military capability and assist the European powers struggling to stop Hitler. This dual goal took on renewed urgency when the German mechanized land forces, supported by the tactical aircraft of the powerful Luftwaffe, rolled through Denmark and Norway on April 9, 1940, then through Belgium, Luxembourg, the Netherlands, and France in May. In a stunning succession of events, the Allies withdrew their troops (principally British) from the European continent in an emergency retreat at Dunkirk, France, in the last days of May; Italy entered the war on June 10; and France capitulated on June 22. After the fall of France and during the crucial year before Hitler turned against the Soviet Union in violation of the nonaggression pact he had signed with the Soviet leader Joseph Stalin in August 1939, Britain, under the leadership of Prime Minister Winston Churchill, stood alone among the European powers to bear the brunt of German aggression. It was also during this year that the United States both lent its support to Britain—its European friend and "neighbor," as Roosevelt liked to say—and clung firmly to its nonbelligerent status. Repeal of the arms embargo in October 1939 was a critical first step toward striking that balance (belligerents could now purchase arms as well as other supplies on a cash-and-carry basis). Roosevelt's appointment of two ardent interventionists and prominent Republicans to his cabinet in June 1940—the former secretary of state Henry L. Stimson as secretary of war and the 1936 vice presidential nominee Frank Knox as secretary of the navy—signaled his determination to win bipartisan support for a course of action that remained extremely controversial. While the exchange of American World War I destroyers for British naval bases in August 1940 was mostly symbolic, the passage of the Lend-Lease Act has rightly been seen as a turning point in allowing Roosevelt to circumvent the restrictions imposed by the Neutrality and Johnson acts. As Roosevelt explained in a radio broadcast in December 1940, when he first suggested the idea, the unorthodox measure would allow the country to provide war material to the Allies unobstructed by "the dollar sign." Its adoption in March 1941 sealed the United States' commitment to the Allies.

President Roosevelt's effort to convince the nation, and Congress, that aid to Britain was in the American interest can be traced through his public speeches and addresses.[3] As Michael Sherry has rightly pointed out, the development of air power, and what the president perceived as the "annihilation of time and space" brought about by new technology, was crucial to his conviction that the oceans no longer provided "adequate defensive barriers." In a message to Congress on May 16, 1940, he urged the building of at least fifty thousand planes a year. The realist tone of his public warnings reflected a keen sense of American vulnerability and a concern that his compatriots were oblivious to the danger. That Roosevelt's preoccupation with national and hemispheric secu-

rity overshadowed his humanitarian impulse is especially noticeable in radio addresses delivered at key moments in the unfolding
European war, on September 3, 1939, and May 10, 1940. The first
was a Fireside Chat, the second a broadcast speech to the delegates
of the Pan American Scientific Congress assembled in Washington.
The right of self-government, the protection of small nations, and
the restoration of peace and democracy abroad, which would figure prominently in the joint declaration of war aims that Roosevelt
and Winston Churchill were to adopt in August 1941, are notice-
ably absent from these addresses. Rather, it was imperative to
"keep war from our own firesides," as the president stated in September. Likewise, on May 10 he warned against the danger that
"forces of arms" present to democracy.

FDR's emphasis was on protecting the Americas, now "the
guardian of Western culture, the protector of Christian civilization," from potential aggressors. "The inheritance which we had
hoped to share with every nation of the world is, for the moment,
left largely in our keeping: and it is our compelling duty to guard
and enrich that legacy, to preserve it for a world which must be
reborn from the ashes of the present disaster." A potential attack
on the Americas represented a new historical possibility, he stressed.
Speaking "in terms of the moving of men and guns and planes
and bombs, every single acre—every hectare—in all the Americas
from the Arctic to the Antarctic is closer to the home of modern
conquerors and the scenes of the attacks in Europe than was ever
the case in those episodes of history that we read about." The same
themes—"the dangers which confront us," the need for "national
protection," the "lightning attacks [that] are a part of the new
technique of modern war," and the imperative "to face the facts
realistically"—dominated the president's address to Congress as
he requested (and was granted) appropriations for national defense in the following days. Still, in his Fireside Chat of May 26, all
that the president could offer to the civilian populations of Eu-

rope who "are now moving, running from their homes to escape
bombs and shells and fire and machine gunning, without shelter,
and almost wholly without food" was compassion, and a Hooverian
call for Americans to give to the Red Cross. This humanitarian
appeal was, according to FDR's biographer Kenneth Davis, "a last-
minute tacked-on preliminary to his prepared text," which, like all
others from this time period, addressed the need for Americans to
ensure their national and hemispheric security, not to assume international responsibility.[4]

In the summer and fall of 1940, President Roosevelt was running for an unprecedented third term. During this unusual campaign, Congress adopted the nation's first peacetime draft, which
Roosevelt's Republican opponent, Wendell Willkie, also supported. The Selective Training and Service Act, which passed by
just one vote in the House of Representatives, was a limited measure and a defensive one: compulsory service was limited to a
maximum of one year, and draftees were to serve in the Western
Hemisphere or in U.S. territories only. These restrictions would
be lifted only after the country entered the war as a belligerent.
For now, it was necessary to "fend off war from our shores" and
"prevent our land from becoming a victim of aggression," stated
Roosevelt on September 16. "It is a program obviously of defensive preparation and of defensive preparation only," emphasized
the president in a radio address delivered on the first registration
day, October 16. This statement was in line with the pledge he
made in his Boston campaign speech of October 30—"Your boys
are not going to be sent into any foreign wars"—and it was reflec-
tive of public opinion, which was still deeply ambivalent about
intervention abroad, even if indirect.

After the November election, Roosevelt assumed a more aggressive posture and pushed Americans to a fuller embrace of
their responsibilities to their British "neighbors," namely, through
the Lend-Lease Act. In the December 17 press conference, when

Roosevelt first discussed the program, the rationale he gave was clearly emphasizing the "selfish"—a term he used three times—interest of the United States in "doing everything to help the British Empire to defend itself." This theme is echoed in his "Arsenal of Democracy" radio address of December 29, Roosevelt's first Fireside Chat following his reelection. He first pressed upon his audience the "undeniable threat" posed by the expansionist and belligerent Axis states: "The Nazi masters of Germany have made it clear that they intend not only to dominate all life and thought in their own country, but also to enslave the whole of Europe, and then to use the resources of Europe to dominate the rest of the world." Then he insisted that indirect intervention through aid to Britain would increase the likelihood the United States could stay out of the war. Throughout the battle over the Lend-Lease Act, Roosevelt continued to press its critical importance for national security rather than international responsibility.

In July 1941, in the introduction he wrote to Samuel Rosenman's published collection of his papers and addresses, the president was blunt about the relative importance he attributed to self-interest in his program of aid to Britain. In words that echoed his May 27, 1941, radio address announcing an "unlimited national emergency," he explained: "The course that the American people have now taken for themselves in their 'all-out' aid to Great Britain and other nations resisting the aggression of dictators, is a course prompted fundamentally by hard-headed self-interest and self-concern. Our policy is not based primarily on a desire to preserve democracy for the rest of the world. It is based primarily on a desire to protect the United States and the Western Hemisphere from the effects of a Nazi victory upon ourselves and upon our children."[5]

As Roosevelt was penning these words, the effects of Nazi occupation were brutally felt by European populations, and especially by the European Jewry, who had been singled out for annihilation by Hitler. Although the "Final Solution" policy of mass extermination would not be officially adopted until January 1942, Jews under Nazi control suffered escalating violence. During the pogroms of the "Night of Broken Glass" (Kristallnacht) on November 9–10, 1938, Jewish homes, synagogues, and businesses were destroyed, ninety-one Jews were murdered, and twenty-six thousand were arrested and deported to concentration camps. Many Jewish families subsequently sought refuge beyond the borders of Greater Germany, which by then included Austria and Czechoslovakia. The Nazi brutality intensified after the invasion of Poland in September 1939 with the forced relocation of Jews to ghettos and labor camps where death by starvation, disease, and beatings took the lives of thousands. With the invasion of the Soviet Union in June 1941, special killing squads began their gruesome work, and by the fall, secret experiments were conducted to devise efficient methods for the mass murder of hundreds of thousands, eventually millions, of Jews. During the critical period between the escalation of violence in 1938 and the fall of 1941, when the Nazi regime stopped issuing exit visas to the Jewish population under its control, the question of how to respond to the refugee crisis posed itself to the rest of the world with pressing urgency.

"The high point of American generosity toward refugees," noted the historian David Wyman, was in the eighteen months between the annexation of Austria in March 1938 and the beginning of the war, when the United States fully used its German and Austrian immigration quotas and provided haven to sixty thousand refugees.[6] On March 25, Roosevelt had called for an international conference on the refugee crisis. Although no substantial action came out of the gathering of thirty-two nations in Évian, France, in July, the president had then pledged to accept refugees up to the quota limits, and despite the unemployment crisis and pressures from restrictionist groups, he momentarily kept his promise. In mid-November, a few days after Kristallnacht, the president also announced in a press conference his administration's decision to renew the visitor's visas of approximately twenty thousand Germans who were in the United States at the time. The event offered a rare instance when the president publicly spoke of his humanitarian obligation to act on behalf of Hitler's victims. "I don't know, from the point of view of humanity," he told reporters, "that we have a right to put them on a ship and send them back to Germany under the present conditions . . . It would be a cruel and inhuman thing to compel them to leave here." More typical of his response to the refugee crisis was the note he scribbled in the margin of a memo asking for his position on the Wagner-Rogers bill for refugee children in June 1939: "File—No Action." The bill, which would have allowed entry to ten thousand Jewish children outside the quota limit in 1939 and again in 1940, died in committee.[7]

More could have been done to assist refugees had the quotas been increased, but Congress and public opinion were explicitly hostile to any relaxation of immigration laws. In the period between 1930 and 1938, the German quota had remained underutilized, partly as a response to economic anxieties. A strong nativist sentiment dating back to the turn of the century and a resurgence of antisemitism in the 1930s further explain the fierce determination to close the golden doors to Jewish refugees in those years. As Deborah Lipstadt has noted, the American press responded with increasing outrage and horror to the mounting evidence of German brutality, and the fact that the violence was directed at the German Jews did not escape notice, but it did not mitigate the strong anti-immigration sentiment. The influential *New York Times*, in spite of its Jewish ownership and readership, buried the news of antisemitic violence in its inside pages.[8] Roosevelt was acutely aware of the nuances in public opinion and limited himself to a policy of small gestures. His pragmatic response, wrote Robert Dallek, an otherwise sympathetic observer of the president's

conduct of foreign policy, amounted to a failure of moral leadership: "It is difficult to escape the feeling that a sustained call by
FDR for allowing Nazi victims to come to the United States in
greater numbers might have mobilized the country's more hu-
mane instincts. It was something that surely must have occurred
to Roosevelt. But his failure to act upon it suggests that the Jewish
dilemma did not command a very high priority in his mind." As
in the case of his decision to support the internment of Japanese
Americans in 1942, saving Jewish refugees from Nazi persecution
"required him to take a stand on grounds of principle against pre-
vailing political, military and/or foreign opinion. But this he would
not do."[9]

In late January 1940, responsibility for the State Department's
visa section was given to Breckinridge Long when he was ap-
pointed assistant secretary of state for special problems. Long, the
former ambassador to Rome, was an antisemite who found *Mein
Kampf* "eloquent in opposition to Jewry and to Jews as exponents
of Communism and chaos." He made it a personal crusade to
completely halt the trickle of refugees to the United States, and he
largely succeeded; in 1940 the quotas of the countries of refugee
origin were only 53 percent filled.[10] As Nazi Germany extended
its control over large parts of Western Europe, a new argument
was added to support increased restrictions on the flow of refugees: national security. As explained by the historian Harry Feingold, the remarkable charge that Hitler's victims could pose as his
agents abroad had gained widespread currency by then. "Why
would the Nazis try to rid themselves of a particularly rich pool of
skilled labor during wartime if not for the purpose of infiltrating
agents into the receiving countries? This line of reasoning, first
heard in London in September 1939, was soon echoed in France,
and became, in 1940, the rallying cry of all those opposed to a
more active rescue effort."[11] It resonated in the American press.
"The fall of Europe was attributed to its having been betrayed by

those to whom it had offered refuge," noted Deborah Lipstadt. Mainstream publications such as *The Saturday Evening Post* carried articles about Nazi agents disguised as refugees; *The New York Times* attributed the fall of Norway to "a fifth column composed of Germans who had been brought to the country orphans after World War I."[12] These arguments were used by Long to legitimize the erection, in the summer and fall of 1940, of "paper walls" that made it all but impossible for refugees to leave Europe. It also explained the regulation adopted in June 1941 that denied a visa to any immigrant who had close relatives in occupied Europe. "According to the Department," noted Feingold, "there was evidence that refugees were being coerced to become agents for Germany by holding relatives as hostages."[13] These arguments were inhumanely absurd, as pointed out by pro-refugee groups at the time, but they continued to underpin public policy.

The concern for national security was central to Roosevelt's public rhetoric and policies in the critical twenty-seven months following the declarations of war in Europe. It infused Roosevelt's public plea for the nation to prepare itself militarily to block the advance of Nazi Germany should Britain fail at the task. The same argument was also used to tighten refugee policies at a time when the victims of Nazi oppression desperately needed to leave the Continent. Only once did Roosevelt come close to suggesting publicly that he embraced the view that Jewish refugees might threaten American national security. In his May 26 Fireside Chat, he warned against "the Trojan Horse. The Fifth Column that betrays a nation unprepared for treachery." The president probably had in mind here his anti-interventionist opponents, who in the summer of 1940 were vigorously challenging his attempt to secure indirect assistance for Britain. But while his intentions may remain unclear, the fact remains that the two salient issues of the pre–Pearl Harbor stage of the war—the need to stop the advance of Hitler and the refugee question—did not receive comparable attention on the part of the president: the former was considered an executive priority, while the latter went ignored by Roosevelt, who was content to leave it to the State Department.

Roosevelt's vision of what was at stake in World War II, as illustrated in his Four Freedoms speech, no doubt included the noble principles of self-determination and defense of human rights. But the democratic and humanitarian rhetoric that came to dominate official representations of the war's goals in 1942 and afterward was not representative of the president's public pronouncements prior to the attack on Pearl Harbor. Of course it should surprise no one that the national interest and security were prominent in Roosevelt's justification of the need to intervene in the European conflict during that time period. Very seldom does a country go to war for altruistic reasons.

## 2

## THE GREAT DEBATE

Prior to the Japanese attack on Pearl Harbor and the Philippines in December 1941, Americans were divided on whether they should intervene in the wars raging in Europe and in Asia. Public opinion polls indicated that less than 20 percent of Americans desired full involvement in the wars abroad. Those who actively campaigned in favor of aid short of war were represented, after May 1940, by the Committee to Defend America by Aiding the Allies, a group that had the support of the White House and was led by the Kansas publisher William Allen White (for which it became known as the White Committee). Also building support for aid to Britain were Edward R. Murrow's live CBS broadcasts of the bombing raids on London in the fall and winter of 1940–1941. Along with Hollywood studios and newsreels producers, all major broadcasters provided full and sympathetic coverage of the war in Europe. Arguing against intervention in international wars were elected representatives from all regions of the country, prominent Americans (including the aviator Charles Lindbergh and the historian Charles Beard), and groups from across the political spectrum (including fascists, socialists, pacifists, and African American leaders). After September 1940, mainstream anti-interventionists rallied behind the America First Committee, which counted 450 chapters and subchapters nationally and a membership of 800,000 to 850,000 by December 1941. Like the White Committee, America First sponsored public rallies and nationwide radio broadcasts, distributed literature, and made speakers available to public interest and neighborhood groups.

The controversy over the role that the United States should play in the conflict was fierce. As President Roosevelt memorably told the White House Correspondents' Association on March 11, 1941, just a few days after the passage of the Lend-Lease Act, "We have just now engaged in a great debate. It was not limited to the halls of Congress. It was argued in every newspaper, on every wavelength, over every cracker barrel in all the land; and it was finally settled and decided by the American people themselves." By then, his opponents had lost the war of public opinion, but, although they were now on the defensive, a large and diverse group of Americans continued to speak publicly and passionately against intervention in the conflict. The debate was temporarily halted by the attack on Pearl Harbor; it resumed after the war, in the late 1940s and 1950s, as many historians who had themselves participated in it assessed Roosevelt's foreign policy.[1] Since the early 1960s, a consensus has emerged in the historical profession on the necessity of intervening on the side of the Allies. But while most historians, along with the general public, will now readily agree that American aid to Britain followed by direct intervention in the conflict was necessary, this judgment, passed with the benefits of hindsight, should not obscure the passion and legitimacy with which Americans debated foreign policy between 1939 and 1941.

As the historian Justus D. Doenecke has most recently documented in *Storm on the Horizon*, no single, unified movement existed to counter Roosevelt's interventionist policies. "The house of anti-interventionism contained many mansions," he wrote, "and the bitterest of enemies might agree on only one premise: the necessity of avoiding full-scale American involvement in World War II. Reasons could be contradictory: opposition to fundamental social reform or fear of radical social change; lack of the needed armament or Jesus's injunctions against 'the sword'; a global analysis that predicted eventual victory of the world's totalitarian powers or one that predicted their defeat." Anti-interventionism was stronger in the Republican Midwest than in other regions, and many Americans of German, Italian, and Japanese descent retained family ties and sentimental attachments that made a war against the Axis undesirable. But the geography of ethnic and partisan loyalty only partly explains the virulent opposition to American belligerency. So it is with ideological persuasion. Pacifists, who by the 1930s had developed a large network of organizations, maintained a deep abhorrence of war, as did the Socialist Party under the vigorous leadership of Norman Thomas. Also hostile to intervention was the nondemocratic right, including the supporters of the popular— and openly antisemitic—Catholic priest Father Charles Coughlin. Between these two extremes, a diverse group of congressmen, intellectuals, public figures, newspaper publishers, and reporters who occupied the mainstream of American public opinion opposed virtually every single step undertaken by the Roosevelt administration to assist, however timidly at first, the nations resisting aggression.[2] The lack of cohesion weakened their effectiveness, but it did not alter their historical significance. Whether the United States should intervene in a world at war was the salient issue of public debates between the invasion of Poland and the attack on Pearl Harbor.

In the heat of the controversy, the "isolationists," as their opponents called anti- and noninterventionists, were accused of being appeasers, Hitler's accomplices, and Fifth Column infiltrators. Among those who publicized these attacks was Theodor Geisel, the author of children's books who is better known as Dr. Seuss. In 1941 he joined the editorial board of the liberal and interventionist newspaper *PM*, and over the next two years he drew more than four hundred political cartoons deriding the head-in-the-sand attitude of his contemporaries. Although scholars have refuted the accusations of disloyalty launched against those opposed to war, they have stuck. "History has not been kind to the anti-interventionists of 1939–1941," noted Doenecke. Mark Stoler concurs: "At best, they have been perceived as simply wrong in their assessment and conclusions; at worst, as ignorant fools and/or Fascist sympathizers. Seldom, if ever, in American history has a major, popular movement been so thoroughly and quickly discredited."[3]

How is this important turning point in American foreign policy, and the controversy that it generated, explained to students? How are those who opposed intervention and their reasons for doing so typically depicted in coverage of the period? A review of seventeen of the most commonly used U.S. history survey texts reveals that treatment of the topic varies, as one would expect, and that it is generally brief; given the space constraint imposed by the genre, this is also somewhat predictable. But most striking is the persistence of stereotypes and misrepresentations in discussions of this subject. To be sure, some texts (about one-third of those analyzed) present well-balanced accounts of the period and invite students to ponder the difficult political and moral choice that belligerency entailed. But overall, the topic is cursorily treated, the anti-interventionist point of view inadequately explained, and its proponents unfairly dismissed as pro-fascist and antisemitic.[4] Although historians have generally been critical of several aspects of the *conduct* of the Good War, most textbooks leave the readers with the impression that the opponents of American entry in the war were terribly misguided and that the debate about whether America should join in the conflict was not entirely legitimate.

The reluctance to intervene in the war was partly rooted in America's deep-seated tradition of nonentanglement in foreign affairs. After World War I, when the United States rejected membership in the League of Nations, it did not "isolate" itself from the rest of the world, but it did embrace what scholars now call a policy of "independent internationalism." During the 1920s, that policy entailed participation in world politics but a strict rejection of multilateral commitments. Unilateralism, in other words, or a "policy of independence in foreign relations which would leave the United States free at all times to act according to the dictates of national self-interest," constituted the preferred course of action.[5] This important period in American foreign policy, which set the stage for America's reluctance to join France and England as they declared war against Germany in September 1939, is comprehensively treated in textbooks, typically and justifiably occupying a full chapter. The following twenty-seven months of American nonbelligerency, however, receive cursory treatment. Partly out of necessity, given the space constraints faced by authors of survey texts, but also reflecting the greater importance given to the nation's spirited defense of democracy abroad during the period of belligerency, examination of the tremendous challenges that the European declarations of war posed to the American policy of nonentanglement is often marked by excessive brevity. Coverage of the opposition to intervention between 1939 and 1941 is not uncommonly limited to a few sentences, and although some brief accounts of the period are accurate and fair, most fail to do justice to the noninterventionist position.[6]

Several texts mention that a debate existed, and often that it was loud and bitter, but they provide little information about its substance. In *Making America*, for instance, Carol Berkin and her collaborators pepper the narrative with mentions of the strength of opposition to any kind of intervention in the European war: "As hostilities began in Europe, isolationism remained strong in the United States"; Roosevelt knew that Churchill's request to secure goods on credit "would face tough congressional and public opposition"; the Lend-Lease proposal "drew the expected fire from isolationists" and Roosevelt "breathed a sign of relief when [it] passed easily." But, except for vague references to the refusal to be dragged into war, the reasons for opposing intervention are left unexplained.[7] Mark Carnes and John Garraty in *American Destiny* and in *The American Nation* similarly mention the existence of opposition to indirect intervention, but its allegedly irrational nature is intimated by the image of "the American people, like wild creatures before a forest fire, rushing in blind panic from the conflagration" or by a "windy burst of isolationist rhetoric."[8] *The American People*, although opening the chapter on "The Twisting Road to War" (1933–1941) with a warning against seeing past events as inevitable and in hindsight, thus summarizes the debate in the summer of 1940: "How should the United States respond to the new and desperate situation in Europe? William Allen White, journalist and editor, and other concerned Americans organized the Committee to Defend America by Aiding the Allies, but others, including Charles Lindbergh, the hero of the 1920s, supported a group called America First. They argued that the United States should forget about England and concentrate on defending America."[9] Likewise, the authors of *The American Promise* devote only a few sentences to explaining why Roosevelt needed to "placate isolationists" and "maneuvered to support Britain." Only in the context of the revision to the neutrality laws in 1939 is this brief explanation of the anti-interventionist position offered: that it protested that "the United States had no business interfering in a European conflict that did not threaten American shores." Although the "heated debate" is mentioned in this case, it is omitted from the section on the Lend-Lease Act.[10] Even when the account is accurate, excessive brevity—especially when bordering on flippancy ("forget about England")—makes it difficult to appreciate the nature of the disagreement over intervention, let alone to explain how the critical events following the invasion of Poland challenged, or reinforced, the deep commitment to nonentanglement held in peacetime.

The aviator Charles Lindbergh was, from September 1939 to December 1941, one of the most outspoken opponents of Roosevelt's aid-short-of-war policies, and he features prominently in textbook accounts of the period. In May 1940, at that critical turning point in the unfolding of Hitler's invasion of western Europe, Roosevelt warned Congress and the public that the Western Hemisphere was at risk of a direct enemy attack. He and especially Secretary of State Cordell Hull were also concerned with economic strangulation should a dictator come to dominate large regions of the world, as was possible then in Europe and Asia. Roosevelt also feared Nazi manipulation of internal dissent in foreign countries, especially but not only in Latin America. But his anxieties over a direct military attack on America were prominent.

In response to President Roosevelt's request for military appropriations, Lindbergh delivered one of his most virulent attacks on Roosevelt's foreign policy. Lindbergh, to the dismay of pacifists, did not oppose the buildup of America's military capability, for he believed that America's defense required it. He shared with Roosevelt a belief in the importance of air power in modern warfare. But, in sharp contrast with the president, Colonel Lindbergh ridiculed the contention that America had anything at risk from Nazi aggression. In a radio address that was nationally broadcast on May 19, three days after Roosevelt's message to Congress, the aviator who had captured the American imagination with his pioneering solo flight across the Atlantic in 1927 directly refuted Roosevelt's contention that aggression was at the nation's doorstep. "From the standpoint of defense, we still have two great oceans between us and the warring armies of Europe and Asia." Speaking as one with an extensive knowledge of air power—Lindbergh had lived in Europe from 1935 to 1939 and observed aviation developments in Germany, France, Britain, and Russia firsthand—he presented an alternative scenario that was as convincing and as "realist" as Roosevelt's, and no doubt more reassuring to Americans:

> Let us not be confused by this talk of invasion by European aircraft. The air defense of America is as simple as the attack is difficult when the true facts are faced . . .
>
> It is true that bombing planes can be built with sufficient range to cross the Atlantic and return. They can be built either in America or Europe. Aeronautical engineers have known this for many years. But the cost is high, the target large, and the military effectiveness small. Such planes do not exist today in any air force. A foreign power could not conquer us by dropping bombs in this country unless the bombing were accompanied by an invading army. And an invading army requires thousands of small bombers and pursuit planes; it would have little use for huge trans-Atlantic aircraft.
>
> No; the advantage lies with us, for great armies must still cross oceans by ship. Only relatively small forces can be transported by air today, and over distances of a few hundred miles at most. This has great significance in Europe, but it is not an element that we have to contend with in America.

America could still rely on its geographic isolation from Europe, the aviator maintained. Yet it should build up its own air force and military personnel, and cultivate hemispheric relationships for additional protection. To do any more, such as sending aid to Britain, was running the unnecessary risk of getting embroiled in "shifting sands of war," not to mention depleting America's own military capability in support of a country whose victory was "extremely doubtful," as he told Congress in a testimony opposing Lend-Lease. To "interfere with the internal affairs of Europe" was detrimental to America's best interest and not essential to its national security. Lindbergh and the America First Committee denied that Hitler sought world conquest, or that the fascist dictator could ever achieve that goal. A "prepared" America, they insisted, was invincible.[11]

This was the central argument made by anti-interventionists to challenge the diversion of American resources to assist European powers. But it was not the only objection to aid short of war. Criticism that the United States would be drawn into a conflict to defend British imperialist interests was voiced by liberal anti-interventionists (and shared, to some extent, by Roosevelt). That exaggerated accounts of German atrocities were used, as they had been during World War I, to draw the nation into the conflict was commonly feared. Finally, there were doubts about whether Britain, and later the Soviet Union, would be able to counter the German attack, hence concerns that scarce American war matériel would be wasted or, worse, fall into the hands of dictators. Dozens of other objections were made, some more legitimate than others. But the opinion that America should remain neutral rather than aid other nations at the cost of being drawn into the conflict continued to be held by a majority of Americans until the fall of 1940. The shift of public sentiment has been thus summarized by the historian Wayne Cole: "As late as May and June 1940, the high tide of German military triumphs in Western Europe, nearly two-thirds of Americans thought it more important for the United States to stay out of war than to aid Britain at the risk of war. But the proportions changed. In August, September, and October, Americans divided almost evenly on the question." By late 1940, a majority supported aid to the Allies as the best chance for peace, even with the accompanying risk of being drawn into the conflict. Acceptance of aid short of war was sealed only with the adoption of the Lend-Lease Act in March 1941. Even after this landmark legislation, however, a vocal minority remained steadfast in its opposition to American indirect intervention.[12]

Both the complex and diverse nature of anti-interventionism

and the question of when public opinion shifted in favor of indirect intervention are unsatisfactorily treated in some texts. One error is to overemphasize the shock of September 1939. Students read in George Tindall and David Shi's *America*, following a discussion of Roosevelt's request for a revision to the Neutrality Act in September 1939 (which was partially granted after six weeks of virulent debate): "Once the great democracies of western Europe faced war, American public opinion, appalled at Hitler's tyranny, supported measures short of war to help their cause." Introducing a false suddenness in the response to "the storm in Europe" renders the narrative inconsistent, as one reads two pages later of "an American public that still held staunchly to the doctrine of isolationism" and of the need for Roosevelt to "disguise [the trading of destroyers for airbases publicly announced in early September 1940] as necessary for defense of the hemisphere." The extensive coverage in the next few pages of the "vigorous" and "bitter" debate that raged over intervention and of the "step-by-step" movement away from neutrality restores historical accuracy to the narrative (as do brief but accurate descriptions of the anti-interventionists' concerns and motivations) but leaves the readers struggling to reconcile the discrepancy between the bold interpretative statement presented early in the section and the description of events that followed.[13] In their texts, Mark Carnes and John Garraty offer an explanation that, while chronologically consistent, is equally confusing with its allusions to different levels of "consciousness" in the determination to defeat Nazi Germany: "The German attack on Poland effected a basic change in American thinking. Keeping out of the war remained an almost universal hope, but preventing a Nazi victory became the ultimate, if not always conscious, objective of many citizens. In Roosevelt's case it was perfectly conscious . . ."[14]

Among textbooks that present well-balanced accounts of

the period is Alan Brinkley's *American History*. The debate between Roosevelt and "the powerful isolationist opposition" in the 1939–1941 period is marked by a brief but careful analysis of their respective positions, conveying the impression of a reasonable disagreement among people of goodwill: "There was never any question that both the president and the majority of the American people favored Britain, France, and the other Allied nations in the contest," he wrote in the context of the 1939 revision of the Neutrality Acts. "The question was how much the United States was prepared to do to assist them." Roosevelt's primary concern for national security is foregrounded (his May 1940 request for defense appropriations is explained by the need "to resist a possible Nazi invasion of the United States"), as is his moderate position of assistance without direct intervention (as opposed to the minority who urged an immediate declaration of war). Brinkley's treatment of the anti-interventionists' position is brief, consisting of an introduction of the major figures and of their opposition to Lend-Lease, but measured and fair: "Isolationists attacked the measure bitterly, arguing (correctly) that it was simply a device to tie the United States more closely to the Allies."[15]

Likewise, *The American Story* and *America: Past and Present* (both by Robert A. Divine et al.) present both sides of the debate about national security in a way that makes each position appear reasonable. That the disagreement gradually dissipated as the situation in Europe worsened provides a clear and plausible explanation for the shift in popular opinion. "Voicing belief in a 'Fortress America,' [Roosevelt's opponents] denied that Hitler threatened American security and claimed that the nation had the strength to defend itself regardless of what happened in Europe . . . The interventionists challenged the isolationist premise that events in Europe did not affect American security . . . In the ensuing debate, the American people gradually came to agree with the interventionists."[16] *The American Pageant* also presents fair and informative coverage of the isolationists; it notes their "sincere" concern for national security, their legitimate criticism of "Roosevelt's secretive and arbitrary methods" in the case of the destroyers-for-bases deal, and the critically democratic debate that accompanied consideration of the Lend-Lease bill: "It was no destroyer deal arranged privately by President Roosevelt. The bill was universally debated, over drugstore counters and cracker barrels, from California all the way to Maine, and the sovereign citizen at last spoke through convincing majorities in Congress." The authors rightly note in this context the popular majority in favor of intervention, even at the risk of war, that existed by the spring of 1941.[17]

David Goldfield and his coauthors in *American Journey* also give careful attention to "the reluctance of most Americans to get involved in World War II." In the section significantly titled "The Dilemmas of Neutrality," the anti-interventionists' "realism" is emphasized ("People who opposed intervention in the European conflict were sometimes called isolationists, but they considered themselves realists who remembered the lessons of World War I") along with the resiliency of the opposition to war ("For more than two years after the invasion of Poland, strong sentiment against intervention shaped public debate") and the importance of concerns for national security ("The aviator Charles A. Lindbergh spoke for many when he argued that the best way to ensure the safety of the United States was to conserve resources to defend the Western Hemisphere"). Set in this context, it makes sense that "Roosevelt had to move slowly and carefully" and "chip away at neutrality, educating, arguing, and taking one step at a time."[18]

Finally, *A People and a Nation* (by Mary Beth Norton et al.) also presents a thorough and sophisticated analysis of the period. Norton's team—which includes the foreign-relations specialist Thomas Paterson, himself the author of a widely used survey text on American foreign relations—presents the debate at home in

the context of an international community making similar difficult moral and strategic choices. While the authors note the short-
sightedness of some of the decisions made at the time, they take
care not to let hindsight interfere with historical assessment. For
instance, in their description of the European powers' response
to the aggressive expansionism of Hitler's fascist Germany, they
write: "Britain and France responded with a policy of appeasement,
hoping to curb Hitler's expansionist appetite by permitting him a
few territorial nibbles. The policy of appeasing Hitler, though not
altogether unreasonable in terms of what could be known at the
time, proved disastrous, for the hate-filled German leader con-
tinually raised his demands." The isolationist sentiment in 1937 is
introduced, likewise, in a way that stresses its reasonable and widespread nature:

> Conservative isolationists feared higher taxes and increased ex-
> ecutive power if the nation went to war again. Liberal isolation-
> ists worried that domestic problems might go unresolved as the
> nation spent more on the military. Many isolationists predicted
> that in attempting to spread democracy abroad or to police the
> world, Americans would lose their freedoms at home. The vast
> majority of isolationists opposed fascism and condemned ag-
> gression, but they did not think the United States should have to
> do what Europeans themselves refused to do: block Hitler. Isola-
> tionist sentiment was strongest in the Midwest and among anti-
> British ethnic groups, especially Americans of German or Irish
> descent, but it was a nationwide phenomenon that cut across so-
> cioeconomic, ethnic, party, and sectional lines and attracted a
> majority of the American people.

The mixed and difficult response to the European declarations
of war is treated with similar care, as a legitimate debate about
foreign policy in which "unprecedented numbers of Americans"

participated. Similarly, the shift of opinion after the fall of France
is presented as a process: "Americans gradually shed their isolationist sentiment. Some liberals left the isolationist fold; it became
more and more the province of conservatives."[19]

As fair and balanced as *A People and a Nation*'s account of the
debate is, the last statement quoted above reinforces a common
misconception. The diversity among those opposing intervention is, as I have discussed at the outset of this essay, one of the
central themes of Justus Doenecke's thorough analysis of anti-
interventionist thought. It is well captured in several texts. For
instance, *Liberty, Equality, Power* (John Murrin et al.) notes the
ideological diversity of those "generally lumped together as 'isolationists'"; it explains that some were pacifists, some political
progressives, some conservatives who sympathized with fascism,
and some who shared Hitler's antisemitism.[20] Divine's texts also
sound this theme: "Such diverse individuals as aviator-hero Charles
Lindbergh, conservative Senator Robert A. Taft of Ohio, socialist
leader Norman Thomas, and liberal educator [and University of
Chicago president] Robert M. Hutchins condemned FDR for in-
volving the United States in a foreign conflict." But to what extent,
as Norton's team suggests, did this ideological diversity erode after the summer and fall of 1940, when a majority of Americans
came to support aid short of war? Did anti-interventionism indeed turn to the right in the fall of 1940 or in 1941?

Historians have noted that, especially after the passage of the
Lend-Lease Act in March 1941, the debate degenerated. "In a fundamental sense," writes James Schneider, "there was no foreign
policy debate after lend-lease. Having established their profound
disagreement on several key premises pertaining to the national
and international situation, the two sides had little to say to one
another . . . They repeated old arguments endlessly and sniped at
the motivations of their opponents." While anti-interventionists

accused Roosevelt of searching for a back door to belligerency, the administration branded its opponents with the worst epithets. As described by Wayne Cole:

> In the course of that torrid contest [over Lend-Lease] Roosevelt was even more successful in destroying the public image of leading isolationists than in reducing their numbers . . . By the time Roosevelt began his third term, isolationists were widely viewed as narrow, self-serving, partisan, conservative, antidemocratic, anti-Semitic, pro-Nazi, fifth columnist, and even treasonous. That image distorted the truth, but it formed nonetheless. Roosevelt and his followers helped create that jaundiced view, and it contributed to the declining status and power of isolationism and isolationists then and later.

In this context of increased polarization, and as a majority of Americans came to accept the possibility of a direct intervention as a likely risk of aid short of war, anti-interventionism lost some support in liberal circles, but it did not became the exclusive province of conservatives.[21] Although labor leaders rallied behind Roosevelt policies and the communist left shifted position after the invasion of the Soviet Union in June 1941, the majority of civil rights leaders, to focus for a moment on this important segment of American liberals, continued to oppose assistance to "so-called democracies" because of their record of imperialism and racism. To be sure, some African American leaders supported intervention, including the political scientist Ralph Bunche, the socialist labor leader A. Philip Randolph, the *Baltimore Afro-American*, and the *Chicago Defender* after October 1940. But, as Daniel W. Aldridge III has noted in his study of anti-interventionism and the African American intelligentsia, theirs was a minority position. On the whole, the black press and key leaders, such as the independent leftist W.E.B. Du Bois and the liberal anticommunist Roy Wilkins (then editor of the NAACP's *Crisis*), virulently spoke against policies leading to war up until the attack on Pearl Harbor.

African American anti-interventionists did not represent the mainstream opposition to aid short of war—America First did. What, then, was America First's ideological orientation? Did it undergo a transformation as the debate became increasingly polarized? Formed in the fall of 1940, the America First Committee was led by General Robert E. Wood of Sears, Roebuck and Company. Wood had a reputation in the business world as an enlightened corporate leader, but, according to Wayne Cole, he was a conservative businessman who attracted to the Committee likeminded individuals from both the corporate and the academic worlds. As Cole notes, "The conservative flavor of America First made liberals reluctant to use it as a vehicle for opposing intervention," and although the Committee tried to diversify its membership in order to increase its respectability, it failed in its effort. Cole noted a slight increase in the liberals' reluctance to be associated with the Committee as the debate grew more acrimonious in 1941—they "were unwilling to risk their future careers by being publicly at the front of the Committee's battle against intervention" (as speakers at events sponsored by it, for instance). It is on this basis that Cole explains that the Committee underwent a "limited shift to the Right." But "the magnitude of this change should not be over-emphasized," he continues. "The group of persons who actually exercised significant influence on Committee policy remained relatively unchanged."[22]

Cole's analysis does not support the claim made in some texts that America First was "arch-conservative."[23] In some cases, assertions of the "ultraconservative" nature of the Committee are accompanied by a mention of the diversity of voices opposing intervention, but not always. Of the three paragraphs that *Out of*

*Many* (John Mack Faragher et al.) devotes to "Isolationism," one explains that it "spanned the political spectrum," with the socialist Norman Thomas standing at one end and the "arch-conservative" America First at the other. The following sentence ambiguously states, "Some America Firsters championed the Nazis while others simply advocated American neutrality," giving the impression of the Committee's acceptance of a moral equivalency between legitimate opposition to war and pro-Nazi sentiments.[24] The Committee's leaders, to the contrary, strove to maintain their credibility by keeping fascists at bay.

One of the turning points in the debate that drove liberals away from America First was Charles Lindbergh's September 11, 1941, speech, delivered at a rally organized by the Committee in Des Moines, Iowa. In this infamous speech, Lindbergh identified American Jews as one of three groups of "war agitators" responsible for drawing the country into the war—the Roosevelt administration and the British being the other two. "Their greatest danger to this country lies in their large ownership and influence in our motion pictures, our press, our radio and our government," he went on to declare. "The leaders of both the British and the Jewish races, for reasons which are as understandable from their viewpoint as they are inadvisable from ours, for reasons which are not American, wish to involve us in the war . . . We cannot allow the natural passions and prejudices of other peoples to lead our country to destruction."[25] The speech, which reproduced contemporary antisemitic stereotypes of Jewish influence and denied Jewish Americans' belonging to or having an interest in "our country," drew a storm of criticism from all sides: interventionists seized the occasion to further attack the motives and respectability of Lindbergh and America First; liberal anti-interventionists distanced themselves from the Committee; America Firsters criticized the aviator for his public relations faux pas; even Senator

Robert Taft condemned Lindbergh for referring "to the Jews as if they were a foreign race, and not Americans at all."

These remarks, although they were the only references to Jews that Lindbergh made during the debate over intervention, reflected the ordinary antisemitism to which Lindbergh, like most of his contemporaries, adhered. "Anti-Semitism was sprinkled widely through noninterventionist ranks," wrote Cole. Yet it represented, in the words of the historian Manfred Jonas, "a minor, if particularly unfortunate, ingredient of the isolationist position." This conclusion has been reasserted in all analyses of anti-interventionism. The Des Moines speech was the only time Lindbergh evoked antisemitic arguments in his two years of public speaking on the question of intervention.[26] The same was true of America First, which attempted to distance itself from crude antisemites such as Henry Ford and Father Coughlin. (Only for a short time, in the fall of 1940, did Ford occupy a position of leadership in America First; he was "dumped," explained Cole, when the Committee tried to attract Jewish leaders to positions of prominence. Likewise, America Firsters were cool to Coughlin.)[27] While it might have been the case, as the authors of *Created Equal* (Jacqueline Jones et al.) wrote, that the aviator's opposition to involvement in the conflict was "fueled" by antisemitism, these sentiments were hardly central to anti-interventionism.[28]

It is perhaps not accidental that texts that stress the immoral nature of anti-interventionism also emphasize the humanitarian and democratic impulses at the heart of America's intervention. In both *Created Equal* and (especially) Eric Foner's *Give Me Liberty!*, Roosevelt's "Four Freedoms" speech is prominently featured (and given added emphasis by including Norman Rockwell's 1943 illustration that popularized the speech).

Since the evolution and contested nature of freedom is the working concept driving Foner's survey text, it is not surprising that he organizes his chapter on World War II around this theme. But to use the Four Freedoms as the backdrop for an explanation of pre-1941 isolationist sentiment is somewhat anachronistic. Foner begins his section titled "Isolationism" with a list of morally bankrupt and profit-oriented reasons for opposing intervention: "Hitler had more than a few admirers in the United States. Obsessed with the threat of communism, some Americans approved his expansion of German power as a counterweight to the Soviet Union. Businessmen did not wish to give up profitable overseas markets. Henry Ford did business with Nazi Germany throughout the 1930s. Indeed, Ford plants there employed slave labor provided by the German government." While these are all facts, they do not constitute a representative sample of the main reasons that motivated anti-interventionism either in the pre-1939 period or after the declarations of war in Europe. The paragraph that follows this in Foner's text brings the reader back to a more conventional focus on the specter of World War I, pacifism, and ethnic allegiances and restores some balance in the narrative, but it does not dispel the aura of illegitimacy created by the leading paragraph. The last section, on post–September 1939 resistance to intervention, limits its discussion of the opposition to a brief mention of America First that, tainting by association, emphasizes the "leadership" of Henry Ford, Father Coughlin, and Lindbergh. Thus juxtaposed against Roosevelt's idealistic formulation of the war's meaning—which did not dominate prior to Pearl Harbor—the alleged moral bankruptcy of the anti-interventionists becomes irrefutable. It is also noticeable that the more immediate national security concern, which figured so prominently in Roosevelt's justification for indirect intervention, is mentioned only in passing in this narrative that stresses the ideological imperative to defeat Nazi Germany.[29]

Students reading texts such as Norton's *A People and a Nation* and a few others will have a keen appreciation of the difficult choice represented by the decision to intervene in the conflict. No moral certainty is projected post facto onto this period, clarifying the right course to follow in response to the beginning of the conflict in Europe. In contrast, the ambiguity of Americans' response is highlighted, as is the critical importance, not merely the vehemence, of the debate: "Because the stakes were so high, Americans vigorously debated the direction of their foreign policy from 1939 through 1941." A balanced portrayal of the debate, while respectful of the legitimacy of anti-interventionist concerns, enhances Roosevelt's stature as a leader who faced both a difficult decision to take the country to war and a genuine lack of consensus rather than portraying him as a cunning and deceptive politician maneuvering around a public incomprehensibly resisting a necessary war.

### TEXTBOOKS REVIEWED IN THIS CHAPTER

Berkin, Carol, Christopher L. Miller, Robert W. Cherny, and James L. Gormly. *Making America*. Fourth ed. Vol. II. Boston: Houghton Mifflin, 2006.

Boyer, Paul S., Clifford E. Clark, Jr., Joseph F. Kett, Neal Salisbury, Harvard Sitkoff, and Nancy Woloch. *The Enduring Vision*. Sixth ed. Vol. II. Boston: Houghton Mifflin, 2008.

Brinkley, Alan. *American History*. Twelfth ed. Vol. II. Boston: McGraw-Hill, 2007.

Carnes, Mark C., and John A. Garraty. *American Destiny*. Third ed. Vol. II. New York: Pearson Longman, 2008.

———. *The American Nation*. Twelfth ed. Vol. II. New York: Pearson Longman, 2006.

Divine, Robert A., T. H. Breen, George M. Fredrickson, R. Hal

Williams, Ariela J. Gross, and H. W. Brands. *America Past and Present*. Seventh ed. Vol. II. New York: Pearson Longman, 2005.

———. *The American Story*. Second ed. Vol. II. New York: Pearson Longman, 2005.

Faragher, John Mack, Mari Jo Buhle, Daniel Czitrom, and Susan H. Armitage. *Out of Many*. Fifth ed. Vol. II. Upper Saddle River, N.J.: Pearson Prentice Hall.

Foner, Eric. *Give Me Liberty!* Seagull ed. Vol. II. New York: W. W. Norton, 2006.

Goldfield, David, Carl Abbott, Virginia DeJohn Anderson, Jo Ann E. Argersinger, Peter H. Argersinger, William L. Barney, and Robert M. Weir. *The American Journey*. Fourth ed. Vol. II. New York: Pearson, 2008.

Jones, Jacqueline, Peter H. Wood, Thomas Borstelmann, Elaine Tyler May, and Vicki L. Ruiz. *Created Equal*. Second ed. Vol. II. New York: Pearson Longman, 2006.

Kennedy, David M., Lizabeth Cohen, and Thomas A. Bailey. *The American Pageant*. Thirteenth ed. Vol. II. Boston: Houghton Mifflin, 2006.

Murrin, John M., Paul E. Johnson, James M. McPherson, Gary Gerstle, Emily S. Rosenberg, and Norman L. Rosenberg. *Liberty, Equality, Power*. Second ed. Vol. II. Fort Worth: Harcourt Brace, 1999.

Nash, Gary B., Julie Roy Jeffrey, John R. Howe, Peter J. Frederick, Allen F. Davis, Allan M. Winkler, Charlene Mires, and Carla Gardina Pestana. *The American People*. Seventh ed. Vol. II. New York: Pearson Longman, 2006.

Norton, Mary Beth, David M. Katzman, David W. Blight, Howard P. Chudacoff, Fredrik Logevall, Beth Bailey, Thomas G. Paterson, and William M. Tuttle, Jr. *A People and a Nation*. Seventh ed. Vol. II. Boston: Houghton Mifflin, 2005.

Roark, James L., Michael P. Johnson, Patricia Cline Cohen, Sarah
    Stage, Alan Lawson, and Susan M. Hartmann. *The American
    Promise*. Third ed. Vol. II. Boston: Bedford/St. Martin's, 2005.
Tindall, George Brown, and David Emory Shi. *America: A Narrative
    History*. Seventh ed. Vol. II. New York: W. W. Norton, 2007.

# 3

## "THE GOOD WAR"

*It is a phrase that has been frequently voiced by men of . . . my genera-*
*tion, to distinguish that war from other wars, declared and unde-*
*clared. Quotation marks have been added, not as a matter of caprice*
*or editorial comment, but simply because the adjective "good" mated*
*to the noun "war" is so incongruous.*
                        —Studs Terkel, *"The Good War"* (1984)

*This book ends on December 31, 1941. Most of the people who died*
*in the Second World War were at that moment still alive. Was it a*
*"good war"? Did waging it help anyone who needed help?*
                        —Nicholson Baker, *Human Smoke* (2008)

"The year . . . 1940," wrote the journalist Tom Brokaw in *The Great-*
*est Generation*, "was a critical time in the shaping of this nation
and the world, equal to the revolution of 1776 and the perils of the
Civil War. Once again the American people understood the magnitude of the challenge, the importance of an unparalleled national
commitment, and, most of all, the certainty that only one resolu-
tion was acceptable." In 1998, when Brokaw's book was published,
an extensive scholarship existed on the virulent disagreements
that divided Americans in the period before the attack on Pearl
Harbor. This historical literature shows that the certitude and
consensus posited by the journalist simply did not exist. Yet the
Second World War remains, in Brokaw's narrative, a war that no
one in their right mind would resist. "At the beginning of a new
decade, 1940, . . . it was clear to all but a few delusional isolationists
that war would define this generation's coming of age."[1]
  Brokaw's purpose was not to trace the halting steps that led

to the national commitment to war but to celebrate the many accomplishments and the important legacy of that generation. The
prolific work of the historian Stephen Ambrose, which enjoys
wide popularity among the general public, belongs on the same
shelf. The citizen-soldiers that Ambrose featured in his books, as
the author put it in *Band of Brothers*, "exemplified everything that
was good about the men in the Armed Forces of the United States
in World War II." They fought "for cause and country" and survived
thanks to the unit cohesion that they developed. Even though
they "were embarrassed by patriotic bombast," he explained in
*Citizen Soldiers*, "they knew they were fighting for decency and
democracy and they were proud of it and motivated by it." In a
book for young readers, *The Good Fight*, Ambrose similarly presents the choices faced by young men in 1941 in simple terms:
"One veteran, when asked what it all meant, said that he felt he had
done his part in turning the twentieth century from one of darkness into one of light. Another said, 'Listen, I was eighteen years
old and had my whole life ahead of me. I had been taught the difference between right and wrong. And I didn't want to live in a
world in which wrong prevailed. So I fought.'" That the book es-
chews debates over intervention prior to December 1941 reinforced the point made by this veteran: that the choice whether to
fight was clear.[2]

The fact that veterans themselves "speak with their own voices
and in their own words" adds authenticity to Ambrose's interpretation. The men of the 101st Airborne Division interviewed for
*Band of Brothers*, explained the author, had a direct say in the telling of their story not only in that they provided a primary source
of information through written memoirs or hours of interviews
with the author but also in that they were invited to comment on
and amend the book manuscript before publication. They offered
"a great deal of criticism, corrections, and suggestions," noted
Ambrose in the acknowledgments. Two veterans "especially have

gone through it line by line. This book is, then, very much a group effort." The truth emerged, explained Ambrose, as a symbiotic relationship developed between the historian and his subject: "We do feel that, through our constant checking and rechecking, our phone calls and correspondence, our visits to the battle sites, we have come as close to the true story of Easy Company as possible." The experience of writing the book, Ambrose tells in a "proud boast," has "made me an honorary member of the company."[3]

The paradigm of the Good War that Brokaw and Ambrose embrace has a long and enduring history. An "obligatory goodness," to borrow the phrase used by the World War II veteran and literary critic Paul Fussell, had already been felt during the war itself as official propagandists exaggerated the nation's democratic virtues and tolerated its antidemocratic tendencies as a matter of wartime expediency. The bitter dissension that surrounded the American involvement in Vietnam in the 1960s was instrumental in shaping a nostalgic view of World War II, as were fiftieth anniversary celebrations of the war's beginning and end in 1989 and 1995. To be sure, much *was* good about the war: fascism had to be stopped; citizens displayed a large degree of unity in their support for the national emergency; the war brought prosperity after a decade of economic recession; and it opened new doors to women and members of racial minorities. Yet there was also much about it that cannot be reconciled with the adjective "good," as Studs Terkel noted as early as 1984. Paul Fussell bitterly concurred in his 1989 book, *Wartime*: "There has been so much talk about 'The Good War,' the Justified War, the Necessary War, and the like, that the young and the innocent could get the impression that it was really not such a bad thing after all." No one who encounters E. B. Sledge's account of his experiences with the marines at Peleliu and Okinawa would get that impression. "We were a bunch of scared kids who had to do a job," Sledge told Studs Terkel. "We were patriots," yet not letting your buddies down "was stronger than flag and country." What Sledge has to say about the particular, and contradictory, reasons why one fought is interesting, but his most powerful message is that the war was inhumane and dehumanizing: "When you get down to the real elemental aspect of it what it's all about was just a matter of survival . . . The war that I knew was totally savage." Fussell, Sledge, and countless others who experienced the war, like those interviewed by Terkel, Brokaw, and Ambrose, tell many different stories—all authentic.[4]

As early as 1992, the historian Richard Polenberg heralded the emergence of a more complex, and complete, historical account of the war: "Yet perhaps the face of the real war, certainly of a different war, is at last beginning to get in the books." Several monographs and surveys have documented that "other" and "different" side of the war, usually without challenging its necessity. A middle ground, one can argue, has been found in much of the scholarly treatment of the war. "The goal of this book," Michael Adams explained in the ironically titled *The Best War Ever*, "is to subject the major aspects of the Good War myth to fresh analysis in the hope of presenting a more realistic picture, one that does not demean the achievement of the United States and of liberal democracy but that at the same time does not diminish the stress, suffering, problems, and failures inevitably faced by a society at war." The revisionist position has made inroads in academic circles, but it has not displaced the myth of the Good War.[5]

Perhaps it is true, as noted by the World War II aviator and literary critic Samuel Hynes, that myths exist so we can live with our past. "Myth . . . it scarcely needs saying, is not a synonym for falsehood; rather, it is a term to identify the simplified, dramatized story that has evolved in our society to contain the meanings of the war that we can tolerate, and so make sense of its incoherences and contradictions." The more we know the past to be senseless, one could deduce from his comments, the more we seek reassuring versions of it. What, then, is the role of personal narratives in the creation and preservation of these myths? They are instrumental in the process of mythmaking, but only some of them leave a mark on our collective consciousness, Hynes also remarked. "Not all of them, to be sure [shape our collective memory]: most narratives, of any war, sit dustily on library shelves, unread partly because they are ill-written and dull, no doubt, but partly because they tell the wrong story, because they don't conform to the myth. Those that *are* read tend to confirm each other . . ."[6]

A narrative that may or may not reshape our myth of World War II, for it "tells the wrong story," is the novelist Nicholson Baker's *Human Smoke*. This provocative work of nonfiction speaks in the voices of a small group of individuals who were instrumental in the unfolding of the century's central tragedy. The entries are kept short; they are presented chronologically, much as they would be in a diary; no chapter breaks or explicitly analytical remarks on the part of the author interrupt the flow. The book reads like the collective journal of a world gone mad. Fittingly, it opens with Alfred Nobel's 1892 remark to a pacifist friend: "Perhaps my factories will put an end to war even sooner than your congresses," said the manufacturer of explosives and soon-to-be founder of the Nobel Prizes. "On the day when two army corps may mutually annihilate each other in a second, probably all civilized nations will recoil with horror and disband their troops." That Nobel's prediction proved wrong is Baker's point—the book's central argument is, more precisely, that civilized nations harvested and enhanced the destructive power of modern weaponry to use it against humanity. Baker approaches the question of the war's "goodness" from a humanitarian perspective. "Did waging it help anyone who needed help?" His answer is an emphatic no. He explicitly states his position at the very end of the volume only, in the afterword: "I dedicate this book to the memory of Clarence Pickett and other

American and British pacifists. They've never really gotten their due. They tried to save Jewish refugees, feed Europe, reconcile the United States and Japan, and stop the war from happening. They failed, but they were right."[7]

Whether those who opposed the war were "right" is a matter of conjecture rather than an argument that Baker can convincingly demonstrate. Because the war was fought, what might have happened had its detractors won their case will never be known. A reviewer's remark—"It seems that he wishes to stir up an argument as much as settle one"—speaks to the main quality of Baker's work.[8] Nazi militarism and violence are described in graphic terms, from the Brownshirts' protest against the antiwar movie *All Quiet on the Western Front* in 1930 to the mass murders on the Eastern Front in 1941. The Jewish residents of the Polish ghetto and other survivors of Nazi atrocities appear in the book not only as victims but as historical actors desperately fighting to survive and to cope with their firsthand witnessing of atrocities. Winston Churchill is a central figure in Baker's narrative—more a villain than a hero. He is antisemitic and violently imperialist, particularly in his willingness to deploy military force against unarmed colonials. He is constantly plotting to develop more powerful weapons of destruction (including chemical ones) and to draw America into the conflict. He is infatuated with air power and deliberately committed to bombing civilians as a means of defeating Hitler's armies. As such, he is the modern warrior par excellence.[9] Franklin Delano Roosevelt also appears in his early days as assistant secretary of the navy and shares many of Churchill's unflattering characteristics. His contribution to the world's descent into madness, aside from his indifference to the plight of refugees, is mostly attributed to his "provocation" of Japanese aggression—another mined terrain that Baker travels without paying too much attention to historians' debates. Such is not his purpose. The book's heroes, in contrast, are pacifists (including the Indian leader Mohandas Gandhi, who consistently sought to apply nonviolent solutions to the impending crisis), American noninterventionists (especially the genuine pacifists; Charles Lindbergh is accurately and disapprovingly characterized as a "Nordic supremacist" and a militarist), and humanitarian workers (such as the former U.S. president Herbert Hoover and Clarence Pickett of the American Friends Service Committee) who tried to assist refugees by sending food to Europe or finding them safe haven in the United States or elsewhere.[10]

The sources from which this collage of voices is gathered are familiar to historians: newspaper articles, public speeches, memoirs and diaries, correspondence and memos, official reports, and the like. The commentaries Baker presents also illustrate facts that are well established in historical scholarship, such as the failure of the liberal democracies to rescue Jewish refugees between 1938 and 1941 and the widespread destruction of civilian populations occasioned by the British (later assisted by the American) bombing. Far more provocative is his argument that waging war *worsened* the lot of those most in need of assistance. This argument is made specifically in relation to the impact that the British naval blockade had on the possibility of Jewish emigration, which, in the summer of 1940, still had the support of German officials. "As soon as ships could travel freely again—in other words, as soon as England made its peace with Germany and stopped blockading ocean traffic—the European Jews would go away, after being stripped of any wealth they might still have. It was all contingent, though, on peace with Churchill."[11] Baker also points to the impact that the blockade had on stopping the sending of food relief to civilians in Nazi-occupied Europe, and the incessant effort on the part of humanitarians to circumvent that formidable obstacle.[12]

The war was fought, and many lives were not saved; indeed, the brutal destruction of civilian populations by both Axis and Allied forces got worse as the conflict escalated. The evidence compiled by Baker powerfully demonstrates the vast and in some cases callous destruction brought about by the militarists of all nationalities. But would *not* fighting the war have saved more lives? We will never know. The counterfactual reasoning on which Baker has to rely in support of the pacifists' position cannot support his contention that they were right. In sum, *Human Smoke* presents a powerful moral challenge, not a historical argument.

# COMMENTARY
## by Robert D. Johnston

From the outset of the book, Murray comes off as a hardheaded realist. She's impatient—radically impatient—with the idea that World War II was some kind of "good war" in which Americans, loving freedom and democracy, rushed to save the world from tyranny. She argues—"bluntly," she admits—that the United States "did not join the war out of a sense of responsibility to the free world." Rather, "democratic and humanitarian principles" played a "decidedly marginal role" in the period from the German invasion of Poland in September 1939 to the Japanese attack on Hawaii in December 1941.

Murray makes a very strong case. First, she is correct to insist on the central importance of the period from 1939 to 1941. Most books about the United States and World War II, glorying in battle after battle, speed through these years, preferring to start with the spectacular and infamous bang of Pearl Harbor. Yet Murray asks us to slow down and look at what policy makers—above all, Franklin Delano Roosevelt—were actually saying about possible American involvement in the global conflict.

Did FDR and his fellow government officials care about Europe's persecuted Jews? Shamefully, hardly at all. Did FDR, who did wish to move the country in the direction of aid to the Allies, speak of a distinctively democratic American mission in the global fight against fascism? Again, not really: FDR spoke much more about national self-interest. The genial president himself had no problem admitting that his approach was "selfish"—meaning that his approach was fundamentally about the protection of the United States, not about saving the world. "Our policy is not based primarily on a desire to preserve democracy for the rest of the world," FDR declaimed. Rather, "It is based primarily on a desire to protect the United States and the Western Hemisphere from the effects of a Nazi victory."

Read FDR's words again, and you'll surely agree that Murray could not have a better quotation than this to clinch her argument. Still, I wonder if her interpretation here needs to be quite so stark. Murray refers at the start and the end of the chapter to FDR's "stirring" Four Freedoms speech of January 1941, in which the president eloquently and idealistically spoke of the fundamental human freedoms of speech and worship, as well as freedom from want and fear. To be sure, this idealistic rhetoric came to play a much greater role after American entry into the war. But while FDR did not emphasize idealism before Pearl Harbor, neither did he repudiate it. In a political culture deeply suspicious of American military in-volvement overseas after the many tragedies of World War I, FDR had to convince Americans that their national self-interest was at stake.

But couldn't such "selfishness" coexist with more generous and more democratic mo-tivations? I tend to think so, both for the president and for the mass of citizens. I can't help but think that Murray pushed her argument so hard not just because she wished to offer a necessary corrective to interpretations that emphasize *only* idealism, but also because she wanted to offer a contemporary political lesson. She concludes the chapter: "Very seldom does a country go to war for altruistic reasons." This is a statement for the ages, particularly in the age of Afghanistan and Iraq. I just wish that Murray had been willing to make her politi-cal point—what appears to be a contemporary antiwar lesson—more explicit.

Caring deeply about the teaching of history, I deeply admire what Murray does in the next chapter. While I do recognize some value in these beasts, I am in general extremely critical of textbooks for their all-too-typical reliance on a singular, authoritative voice. Yet as Murray reveals by closely examining how the best textbooks on the market tell the story of isolation-ism in the pre-1941 period, there are actually many stories to tell about this topic—and also many falsehoods and distortions. Murray shows that some textbooks do understand isola-tionism well—as a diverse, reasonable, and strong current in American political culture. But many textbook authors—among them some extremely prominent historians—simply mess things up, trying to make isolationism into a dangerous, irrational, monolithic, and marginal movement.

I'm utterly convinced by Murray here. More generally, it's critical that students, along with scholars, start critiquing textbooks in this manner. Here, I just wish that Murray had gone further. Why, I wonder, do some textbooks get it right, and some so wrong? Is it laziness and a resulting sloppiness? A failure to keep up with recent scholarly interpretations? Or: perhaps politics is involved. For example, the book that Murray most criticizes, *Give Me Liberty!*, is written by a staunch (and deservedly celebrated) leftist historian, Eric Foner, who comes out of a political tradition in which forthrightly fighting the fascists was the only proper moral choice. In general, I would love to have seen Murray try to get under the skin of the historians she is exploring.

Although Murray writes in a calm, measured voice, she concludes the opening section with the moral equivalent of an incendiary device. She starts out by showing that scholars increasingly view the glib newsman Tom Brokaw as the enemy—there was no simple "good war" (a concept that has earned Brokaw much fame and money). Rather, World War II—as does any war—involved a morally ambiguous and complex set of choices to be made in the context of ghastly death and violence. That's a reasonable enough argument, but then Murray introduces Nicholson Baker's *Human Smoke* into the conversation. Baker is not searching for complexity; he wants to completely exterminate our idealism. In his view, World War II was nothing more than systematic rotten murder.

Murray is right to present Baker's terribly important argument, to ensure that such a contrarian view gets into our line of sight. But the way she does so is somewhat akin to throwing a grenade into a foxhole and running like hell. She notes that *Human Smoke* "presents a powerful moral challenge," but she consciously chooses "not to take a position forcefully in favor or against." On the one hand, Murray's refusal to take sides is admirable, as it really does provide room for all her readers to decide for themselves the value of this line of thinking. On the other hand, Murray is a smart and sensitive guide, and I continue to wonder what she really thinks about the ultimate value of Baker's argument—and, by extension, "the Good War."

Part Two

TO "CREATE A WILL TO WIN"

▼

The attack on the American naval bases at Pearl Harbor and in the Philippines on December 7, 1941, silenced the opponents of intervention. Americans threw themselves into battle with eagerness. However, in the summer and early fall of 1942, in the wake of continuing defeats in the Pacific, a slump in public support for the war worried political and military leaders. This was expressed, for instance, in March 1942, when the army chief of staff, General George Marshall, and the chief of the Morale Branch of the War Department, Brigadier General Frederick Osborn, issued directives to the filmmaker Colonel Frank Capra to "create a will to win by . . . showing clearly that we are fighting for the existence of our country and all our freedoms."[1] The desire to fight for and to serve the country, which had been so powerfully galvanized by the Japanese raids on American overseas territories, could not be taken for granted. Thus a formidable and varied body of propaganda material was produced to maintain popular enthusiasm for a long war fought on distant shores. This material offers a window on America's political culture in wartime.

As in the first chapter of part I, a body of primary documents—in this case, propaganda posters—is used to draw out the paradoxes at the heart of wartime culture in chapter 4. Chapter 5 offers a critical review of the work of the historian Robert B. Westbrook to flesh out his interpretation on a related topic. As readers will note, our readings of similar material differ somewhat. The divergence of interpretations is partly a result of the differing questions that motivated our historical quest. My essay on the messages conveyed in the posters reads as it was conceived: as an effort to identify the main messages that these posters conveyed. Because the body of readily available posters is vast and their messages multiple, my argument is broad and somewhat diffuse. Westbrook's stated reason for studying similar propaganda material was to support a particular interpretation about the essentially "privatized" nature of American political culture. Skeptical of Westbrook's interpretation from the outset, I returned to the sources and discovered a more complex historical situation. However, the relationship between primary sources and interpretation is a delicate one, and some readers may be inclined to side with Westbrook's conclusions instead of my own. Interpretation usually develops in tandem with an immersion in the historical record, but almost invariably, historians' own intellectual journeys will color their reading—and selection—of the sources.

The last chapter in this section is a topical essay on the gendered nature of wartime political culture. A fairly conventional type of historical writing, this format relies primarily on secondary sources; unlike historiographical writing, the focus of attention here is not on historians' interpretations as much as on historical events themselves. In this case, the "events" covered fall under the rubrics of social and cultural history; they include women's participation in the war effort and the meanings that they, and their society, drew from that participation.

# 4

## "IT'S EVERYBODY'S JOB"

On a commission by the United States Army, the acclaimed film-maker Frank Capra produced the documentary *Why We Fight*, a seven-episode series conceived to sustain the morale of the troops by explaining the purpose for which the country was at war. In the first episode, *Prelude to War*, which was released to new recruits in October 1942 and to theater audiences in May 1943, Capra dramatically emphasized the totalitarian nature of fascist Italy, Nazi Germany, and "fanatical" Japan. In sharp contrast to the regimented "masses" of "the slave world" he presented the citizens of "the free world" as self-reliant individuals who, through their initiative and courage, would triumph over "the forces of evil." As Kathleen M. German has noted, the series exploited the value of individualism by stressing common themes: "The individual is fighting the massive Nazi military machine; the battle is being waged heroically in the streets and workshops of common citizens; and a free people cannot be subjugated by a regimented people. Each of these themes assumes that initiative and action are paramount in defeating evil aggression."[1]

Also produced for the troops under Capra's direction between 1943 and 1945, the short animated cartoon *Private Snafu* similarly affirmed the importance of individual responsibility to the success of the war, although through a language of comic inversion. These short animated cartoons—they ran about three minutes— were included in the *Army-Navy Screen Magazine*, a twenty-minute collection of newsreels and special features that was released twice a month and shown to servicemen before a Hollywood feature film. Most of the twenty-six cartoons were written by Theodor Geisel, who, after leaving *PM* magazine in early 1943, served in the Army Signal Corps under Capra. As described by the film historian Eric Smoodin, "The point of most of the cartoons in the 'Snafu' series was to show soldiers what would happen when an ordinary recruit did not do his job." Snafu's incompetence and irresponsibility, bred from discontent, led to nothing but disaster for himself (he gets diarrhea because he refuses to wash his mess gear or dies from malaria after ignoring proper measures), his fighting buddies (his platoon falls under Japanese attack because he was too lazy to practice his drills), and, by extension, the successful conduct of the war. The lesson the servicemen were to learn from Snafu's misadventures was that the personal commitment and responsibility of even the most modest private were critical to the war effort.[2]

Capra's wartime work is representative of the broader body of propaganda material produced during the war to maintain the morale of both combatants and civilians. The War Department's Morale Branch was active throughout the war, sponsoring films and printed material for the troops' required orientation courses. In October 1941, the Office of Facts and Figures (OFF) was created to "inform" the public about the issues at stake in the conflict. It was replaced by the Office of War Information (OWI) in June 1942. In addition to these governmental agencies and to all the branches of the Armed Forces that produced propaganda material for recruitment purposes, private corporations and labor unions encouraged the war effort to demonstrate their contribution to the national emergency. Commercial advertisers and artists, independent of their work for the various governmental, military, and private campaigns, also created and exhibited war art through the nation's museums. The body of material produced through this concerted effort constitutes a window into wartime popular culture.

Under the leadership of the poet Archibald MacLeish, the governmental propaganda agencies attracted a group of liberal intellectuals committed to the defeat of fascism. Among the works produced by the OFF and the OWI in the first year of the war was John Philip Falter's *This World Cannot Exist Half Slave and Half Free*, a poster that echoes Capra's contrast between the forces of good and evil. In grim tints of reddish brown, gray, and black, the image depicts a minister and a family backed against a brick wall in the shadow of a soldier whipping a woman. In their eyes one can read anger, even determination to fight back, rather than fear—this message is reinforced by the text printed on the bottom of the poster: FIGHT FOR FREEDOM, or, in other renditions of the same poster, SACRIFICE FOR FREEDOM. Also answering in his own way the question that informed Capra's work, the Lithuanian-born Jewish artist Ben Shahn created images that remain moving to this day. *This Is Nazi Brutality* shows a man dressed in a black suit with his face covered by a cloth and his wrists chained; he stands in front of a brick wall. The text of a broadcast, which relates the horrific events of the Lidice massacre of June 10, 1942, is printed on the poster:

RADIO BERLIN. – IT IS OFFICIALLY ANNOUNCED: – ALL MEN OF LIDICE – CZECHOSLOVAKIA – HAVE BEEN SHOT: THE WOMEN DEPORTED TO A CONCENTRATION CAMP: THE CHILDREN SENT TO APPROPRIATE CENTERS – THE NAME OF THE VILLAGE WAS IMMEDIATELY ABOLISHED. 6/11/42/115P.

Like Capra's films, Shahn's poster uses a creative combination of factual information and emotional appeal to galvanize Americans to action.[3]

Shahn's work is typically associated with the "strategy of truth" that dominated the governmental agencies in the early stages of the war. MacLeish's intellectuals and artists were convinced that only "honest facts about the struggle," rather than the "ballyhoo methods" of modern advertising, were the appropriate and most effective way to sway public opinion behind the war effort. But their crusade to let the facts speak by themselves was short-lived. In April 1943 they collectively resigned, disheartened by what they perceived as the cheapening of the war by the growing dominance of admen's selling techniques in the work of the OWI. As the graphic artist Francis Brennan put it in his resignation letter, he was leaving because of the agency's attempt "to make necessary civilian actions appear palatable, comfortable, and not quite as inconvenient as Guadalcanal." One image, which offended by its superficiality, was a poster produced in 1943 to encourage conservation efforts. It features a young girl and her mother happily canning food, oblivious to the reality of wartime deprivation: "We'll have lots to eat this winter, won't we Mother?" asks the girl innocently.[4] Posters such as this one incensed the liberal propagandists. As Frank Fox has written, "In shock and dismay, [the liberal intellectuals] stood by helplessly as Ben Shahn's chilling depictions of Nazi brutality were discarded in favor of Norman Rockwell's homey Four Freedoms posters." Left in the hands of advertising experts who sold the war as one sells Coca-Cola, wartime propaganda, necessary to rally the public to the worthy defense of freedom, had been degraded to the point of irreverence.[5]

This conventional narrative is, in significant respect, accurate. Images such as Shahn's are rare compared to the upbeat representations of American civilians' contribution to the war effort produced by advertising professionals and commercial illustrators.

But the admen's work, which may be seen now as trite, still deserves scrutiny.

Posters fundamentally transformed the visual environment of wartime America. They were produced in a variety of formats, ranging from single sheets to twenty-four-sheet billboards, and were distributed widely and strategically. As William L. Bird, Jr., and Harry R. Rubenstein have noted in their fine analysis of World War II posters, governmental officials were deliberate in their use of this particular propaganda tool, as they were with all propaganda material.

> As one U.S. Office of War Information (OWI) official put it, "We want to see posters on fences, on the walls of buildings, on village greens, on boards in front of the City Hall and the Post Office, in hotel lobbies, in the windows of vacant stores—not limited to the present neat conventional frames which make them look like advertising, but shouting at people from unexpected places with all the urgency which this war demands." "Ideally," another confirmed, "it should be possible to post America every night. People should wake up to find a visual message everywhere, like new snow—every man, woman and child should be reached and moved by the message."

The propagandists accomplished this goal through an elaborate network of volunteer organizations that placed posters in every public venue imaginable. As further explained by Bird and Rubenstein,

> At the local level, OWI arranged distribution through volunteer defense councils, whose members selected appropriate posting places, established posting routes, ordered posters from supply catalogs, and took the "Poster Pledge." The "Poster Pledge" urged volunteers to "avoid waste," treat posters "as real war ammunition," "never let a poster lie idle," and "make every one count to the fullest extent."[6]

As reflected by their intended target ("every man, woman and child") and by their distribution network based on the voluntary contribution of ordinary Americans, the posters emphasized the individual commitment of each and every American to the war effort. They played on a range of emotions and employed a variety of visual and textual techniques to carry their message. Like that conveyed by Capra, Falter, and Shahn, it was unmistakable: the war was fought for the defense of democratic values, for the defense of America and the free world, and one's individual commitment to the collective effort was critical to its success. As simply stated on a poster designed by artist McClelland Barclay for the National Association of Manufacturers: DEFEND AMERICAN FREEDOM: IT'S EVERYBODY'S JOB (figure 1).[7]

Figure 1

To say that the mobilization of each and every American was at the core of wartime public discourse requires several qualifications. First, it should be noted that the emphasis on the individuality of wartime sacrifice did not obscure the essentially collective purpose that it was meant to serve. As Lawrence Samuel has noted in his study of the war bond campaigns, "National unity—the idea that Americans were joined together for a common purpose—gave larger meaning to the selling of war bonds." This message was prominently conveyed in the poster design that featured the flag and a quote from President Roosevelt, printed in block letters: WE CAN . . . WE WILL . . . WE MUST! Produced as part of the 1942 bond campaign, this image that evoked the nation's collective determination was displayed as billboards at more than thirty thousand locations across the country, and four million copies were printed in small color format.[8] Equally representative of this emphasis on the collective effort is the well-known Iwo Jima flag-raising picture. When used in the Treasury's 1945 bond tour, the image was accompanied by the slogan "Now All Together." As the historian George Roeder has noted, the image "presents the war as a collective effort that nonetheless allows recognition of individual achievement." Although the identity of the servicemen was not immediately evident from Joe Rosenthal's famous photograph, the propagandists considered it crucially important that it be established. In his study of writing for and about the troops, Benjamin Alpers similarly noted that an emphasis on the individuality and autonomy of each American serviceman coexisted with the intrinsic collective and regimented aspects of the military experience. This is apparent, for instance, in the popularity of the team metaphor, which "acknowledged individuality while suggesting that individual attainment gained meaning only in relation to the group."[9]

Just as wartime propaganda presented individuality and collective purpose as compatible, it asserted that differences among individuals and among groups need not be sacrificed to unity. Relying on techniques of market segmentation, the bond drives targeted specific groups, such as unionized workers, white ethnic communities, and African Americans, with material tailored to these particular audiences. Yet the message to all was the same:

service to the nation was essential to the war effort. This pluralist theme—that Americans of different classes, races, and genders could be united on behalf of the nation without losing their individual and group identity—was expressed in a variety of posters: factory workers and businessmen joined Uncle Sam in a handshake in *Together We Win*; an African American and a white man work together in *United We Win*; men and women purposefully walk in the same direction in *Every Man, Woman and Child Is a Partner*. For the purpose of "morale building," if nothing else, differences among Americans were acknowledged but subordinated to the greater goal of national unity.[10]

Several other rhetorical strategies were used by the propagandists to remind the public—sometimes explicitly the male public—of their patriotic obligation. The theme of protection was common, as in *Don't Let That Shadow Touch Them* (figure 2), which features

Figure 2

children whose playing has been interrupted by the shadow of a swastika—the oldest looks apprehensively at the sky while protectively placing his hand on the youngest. Other images similarly associated the war effort with the protection of loved ones: "Ours, to fight for," proclaimed the slogan used on the reproduction of Norman Rockwell's famous *Freedom from Want* and *Freedom from Fear* for the 1943 bond campaign. According to the historians Frank W. Fox and Robert B. Westbrook, the protection of the family was a central theme of wartime propaganda.[11] But patriotic service was not exclusively motivated by appeals to familial obligations. Calls for individuals to protect the nation and the freedoms for which it stood through simple, unadulterated appeals to patriotic sentiment abound. Such was the case of the recruitment poster McClelland Barclay designed for the navy that specifically enjoined Americans to "Arise" in defense of "Your Country and Your Liberty" (figure 3).

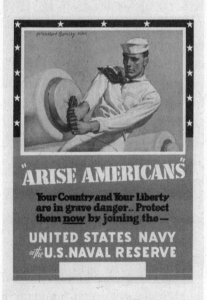

Figure 3

Not only was James Montgomery Flagg's World War I recruitment poster *I Want You* reissued in 1941, but Uncle Sam's pointed finger—which was used by the marines for recruitment purposes in *The U.S. Marines Want You* and by the General Electric Company to encourage industrial production in *Are You Doing All You Can?*—personalized the call for patriotic service without resorting to private obligations.[12]

Given the importance of industrial production to the American war effort, one would expect representations of workers to be fairly common. Similarly, the small-investor focus of the bond program lent itself to a prominent featuring of the ordinary producers in fund-raising propaganda. As Samuel has documented, Secretary of the Treasury Henry Morgenthau deliberately used the bond program to reach out to the working class, by instituting a payroll deduction program, for instance; organized labor responded favorably by actively encouraging its members to purchase bonds. Congruent with Morgenthau's intentions was J. Walter Wilkinson and Walter G. Wilkinson's design for the 1942 bond campaign, *Wanted—Fighting Dollars* (figure 4), which, as Bird and Rubenstein have noted, "idealized the American bondholder as a ruddy-faced workman in bib overalls." Revealingly, the title of the original illustration used for this poster, *I'm No Millionaire, but—I Own a Share in America*," had explicit populist connotations.[13] The workers' cap, which was donned by the Wilkinsons' bondholder, was also featured in Barclay's Uncle Sam in *Defend American Freedom* (see figure 1).

In contrast with the Wilkinsons' bondholder, whose red cheeks and lips gave him a soft, almost feminine appeal, several representations of manual workers emphasized a virile masculine individuality. The manly worker, a figure common in New Deal art, was ubiquitous in *Free Labor Will Win, Let's All Get "Steamed Up," American Labor . . . Producing for Attack*, and the towering *Pour It On!* (figure 5). Of course, the crucial importance of women to the

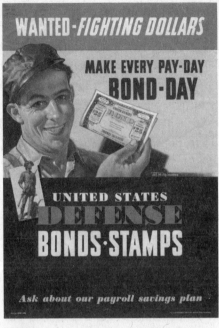

Figure 4

Figure 5

war industry demanded that "manly men" share the stage with patriotic women; hence, in a wartime adjustment to gender stereotypes, Rockwell's famous *Rosie the Riveter*, like the otherwise feminine figure in J. Howard Miller's *We Can Do It!* for Westinghouse, sported strong biceps muscles. The femininity of female patriots was preserved by the trimmed eyebrows, mascara-elongated eyelashes, flushed lips, polished nails, and other softer attributes. Like the valorous fighting men represented in Barclay's portraits of sailors in *Man the Guns* (figure 6) and *Dish It Out with the Navy!* the physical strength associated with manual labor—in the civilian workforce or in the military—was a powerful symbol of individual wartime service.[14]

Also used as a major source of inspiration to mobilize civilians to do their share for the war effort was the sacrifice of servicemen, who were typically represented in small groups or singly. Rhetorically conflated with the battlefield experience was the civilians' contribution through the purchase of war bonds or other home-front activities such as the recycling of scrap metal or fat. Hence, one could "Attack Attack Attack" or, less literally, "Keep him flying!" by buying war bonds. Conservation efforts were portrayed in the same light, as an extension of the battlefront. In *Save Waste Fats for Explosives*, fat dripping from a skillet is equated with bombs falling from the sky. Individual agency is introduced discreetly in this poster, through the feminine hand holding the skillet. The equivalence of sacrifice was explicitly posited in a poster produced for the Second War Loan that proclaimed "They give their lives, you lend your money." Also stressing an essential commonality of purpose between civilians and servicemen were images such as *Men Working Together!* in which a soldier, factory worker, and sailor stand shoulder to shoulder or GM's *Let's All Pull Together!* which depicts a military man, a businessman, and a worker raising the flag. That men were fighting on the battlefront

Man the
GUNS
Join the NAVY

Figure 6

was considered sufficient justification for every civilian to offer his or her sacrifice on the home front.[15]

The conflation of the worlds of civilians and soldiers was possible only because of the sanitized view of the war that dominated the first twenty months of the American involvement. On December 19, 1941, an Office of Censorship was formed, and it worked closely with the War Department to keep combat zone photographs from being released to the public; these censored images were kept in a file labeled "Chamber of Horrors" held in the Pentagon. In September 1943, however, the administration was concerned with what the Office of War Information referred to as the "Over-the-Hump Psychology." In order to keep the home front motivated, photographs that depicted more truthfully the reality of war were carefully released to the public. The first photograph of dead soldiers—featuring three corpses on Buna Beach in New Guinea—appeared in *Life* in September 1943. According to the historian James Kimble, Treasury staffers noted the effectiveness of these more inflammatory images and drew a lesson from it: as one could read in a report on the third loan drive, which coincided with the release of this photograph, "the only way to sell more bonds—indeed to speed the entire war effort—[is] to get the facts of the war to the American people honestly and brutally . . . [and] without gloves on." In its copy guide's suggestion of January 1944, the Treasury outlined the new approach: "Thrust home the stark, realistic picture of what is physically happening to our own men in battle."[16]

The next three drives, all conducted in 1944, featured increasingly strident propaganda. In one ad produced for the fourth drive an American soldier could be seen lying on the ground, blood pouring from his forehead, his body contorted: "When you go home tonight . . . think of a boy who never will . . . ," read the headline. "I Died Today . . . What Did *You* Do?" read a 5th War Loan ad. Several posters depicting dead servicemen echoed the same theme, notably "What Did *You* Do Today . . . for Freedom?" Most remarkable among the material produced toward the end of the war was a poster issued by the navy's Industrial Incentive Division in 1945. Designed by John Falter, also the creator of *This World Cannot Exist Half Slave and Half Free*, *A Strange Sort of Prayer* (figure 7) depicts a soldier kneeling in an abandoned combat field surrounded by discarded pieces of equipment, including what appears to be the boot of a dead comrade. His prayer is euphemistically suggestive of the reality of war: "Me down here, with a burning sun, a mess of insects, too much ocean, and other buddies just as lonely as me . . . And tomorrow and tomorrow I'll still be dodging bullets, still feeling lost in the middle of the night." It expresses a yearning for the war to end: "Oh, God, how nice it must be back home, with Germany licked, and the folks humming, and some of the boys all finished with the fighting." It closes with a desperate plea for civil-

Figure 7

ian support, which was, after all, its purpose to cultivate: "But say, if You can only get the people back home to remember me, maybe they'll still bear down. Maybe they'll still send us their blood, still stay on the job, still keep making the stuff we need." Although the false congruence between the battlefront and the home front had been abandoned, the relevance of civilians' action, or negligence, was still directly linked to the fate of servicemen.[17]

Just as depictions of the reality of war became more graphic as the conflict dragged on, so did representations of the enemy. In 1942, Ben Shahn's explicit emphasis on Nazi brutality had been shunned in favor of upbeat appeals to public support. Hence, in the early stage of the war, the enemy was represented indirectly, by a shadow, for instance, or figuratively, as an arm with the Nazi swastika on its sleeve stabbing a Bible. Also common were caricatures that derided the Axis powers' invincibility by poking fun at their leaders. As the historian Kimble has noted, this reluctance to depict the enemy in anything but the vaguest terms was deliberate.

The public, according to the political marketing expert, Peter Odegard, who advised the Treasury, was "wary of attempts to put Hallowe'en villain-masks on such 'ordinary' people as Hitler, etc.; even genuine documented atrocity tales smack to them of propaganda." In 1944, however, at a time when the administration was also releasing news of atrocities committed by the Japanese against American and Allied forces (during the 1942 Bataan Death March, for instance), the Treasury expanded its use of enemy imagery. As John Dower has shown in his masterful study of racial perceptions in World War II, the Japanese enemy was typically represented as brutish or even verminlike. The desire to awaken sagging public morale had brought America back with a vengeance to the previously discarded strategy of the liberal propagandists.[18]

Governmental agencies as well as private corporations and advertisers used posters, along with other media, to mobilize the nation's support for a fight taking place oceans away from its shores. As one would expect of propaganda, the material produced to sustain the war effort was at odds with the reality of wartime brutality and sacrifice, and it conveyed messages that were internally inconsistent. The latter, more particularly, is worth emphasizing. Appeals to individualist values coexisted with glorification of the collective effort, just as claims to citizens' private (mostly familial) obligations competed with assertions of their public obligations. As the historian Mary Poovey has argued in another context, the work of constructing ideology (or "ideological work," as she puts it) is fundamentally incoherent.[19] Wartime American patriotism is no exception.

# 5

## A MATTER OF PRIVATE OBLIGATIONS?

In two provocative and influential essays on wartime political culture, the historian Robert B. Westbrook examines the cultural and personal forces that motivated American men to serve their country.[1] His study, which constitutes one of the most systematical analyses of American patriotism during World War II, takes as its focal point wartime propaganda and the nature of Americans' felt obligation to their country—what he calls "popular patriotism." Propaganda reveals more than the views of propagandists, he notes; it provides a window into the political culture of a society. Wartime political culture, he argues, is characterized by an impoverished, privatized definition of individual rights that leaves little room for a felt sense of public obligation. What interests Westbrook most is what wartime patriotism reveals of American civic and political culture: "what binds us to (or alienates us from) our nation-state."[2] In essence, Westbrook argues that because of the preeminence of liberalism in midcentury America, and given the universalism of its core values, Americans lack the ability to sustain meaningful civic and national obligations. Key liberal values such as individualism make for a "thin sense of political community,"[3] he explains, while the oxymoronic nature of the American creed, which posits universal values as its own, hampers the formulation of "national" values for which to fight. During World War II, contends Westbrook, the appeal to "private, nonpolitical moral obligations" filled the void left by liberalism.[4] Hence Americans did not fight out of a *patriotic* commitment to the nation, but in the defense of "transnational values . . . and nonpolitical obligations."[5]

Westbrook's argument about the "privatized" nature of Americans' sense of obligation is inspired by Michael Walzer's essay "The Obligation to Die for the State." Walzer's analysis of the impossibility of a genuine sense of political obligation in a liberal society is too complex to review in detail here—but, simply put, following the logic of the seventeenth-century English philosopher Thomas Hobbes, Walzer argues that individuals cannot be expected to die for a state that they created in the first place for their own protection. "A man who dies for the state defeats his only purpose in forming the state . . . A man who risks his life for the state accepts the insecurity which it was the only end of his political obedience to avoid . . . Hence there can be no political obligation either to die or to fight."[6] The state is, in Hobbesean theory, merely an instrument and as such has no claim on citizens' obligations. In the absence of politically logical reasons to die or to fight, service to the state, particularly in time of war, must be sought through other, nonpolitical mechanisms. As Walzer further explains, "Moved by love, sympathy, or friendship, men in liberal society can and obviously do incur ultimate obligations. They may even find themselves in situations where they are or think they are obligated to risk their lives to defend the state which defends in its turn the property and enjoyment of their friends or families. But if they then actually risk their lives or die, they do so because they have incurred private obligations which have nothing to do with politics."[7] It is this argument that Westbrook applies to the World War II period:

Yet what is most striking about propaganda for the "Good War" . . . is the degree to which proponents openly attempted, as Walzer's arguments suggest they might, to exploit private obligations to convince Americans to serve the cause of national defense. Such obligations—to families, to children, to parents, to friends, and generally, to an "American Way of Life" defined as a rich (and richly commodified) private realm of experience— were tirelessly invoked in the campaign to mobilize Americans for World War II, and they formed the centerpiece of the propaganda produced by the state and its allies in Hollywood, the War Advertising Council, and elsewhere.[8]

The historical evidence that Westbrook cites to support his argument is familiar to students of wartime propaganda. As revealed in Frank W. Fox's classic study of wartime advertising and in Allan M. Winkler's history of the Office of War Information, professional advertisers endeavored to "sell victory" by "selling America to Americans," as one executive described the thrust of the industry's wartime goal. This was done through a "tactic of emotional excess." Through pages and pages of supercharged, melodramatic advertisements published in the nation's magazines, and some reproduced as posters, admen put forth their own answer to the question of "why we fight." Fox writes that they "self-consciously came to promote a coherent view of what the war was all about, why the United States was involved in it, and what the significance of an American victory would be." In that version, the defense of democratic freedoms was accomplished through battles that were "suffused with excitement and adventure" against enemies who were "hateful, despicable creatures" or, conversely, "a mere caricature of evil in which the demonic and satanic were so overdrawn as to become comic." Most important, Fox describes how victory became associated with the triumph of an "American Way of Life"

defined through the home, the family, and the Good Life provided by private enterprise. "We fight for the right to come back
to our homes, our America, our way of life," whispers a Marine in
an ad produced for the Corps.[9]

Westbrook's reading of wartime culture echoes Fox's analysis.
He notes the text of a Community Silverplate ad: "These are the
things we are fighting for . . . That our children may look to the skies
in joy and confidence . . . and not in fear."[10] Also illustrative of this
theme is a Dixie Cups ad that features the daughter of a civilian air
raid warden looking at a young flying officer: "He won't let them
hurt us . . . will he, Mommy?" she anxiously asks. Less obvious but
also revealing is a Philco ad featuring Uncle Sam—a composite
state and family figure—protecting the home of "Our Democratic
Institutions" from "Vandals" (the Axis leaders). Faithful to his
Hobbesean theme, Westbrook notes: "The Philco ad . . . provides a
nice example of how the liberal state could represent itself as a family relative, 'Uncle Sam,' to obscure the fact that a declaration of war
meant that it had failed to hold up the bargain struck with its citizens to protect them from death in exchange for their obedience. It
was not Uncle Sam that was protecting the family during the war
but fathers, mothers, and other relatives who went to war to keep
Hitler, Mussolini, and Tojo from the door, and it was their private
obligation to do so that the American state mobilized."[11]

Westbrook adds to Fox's analysis of wartime advertising a close
reading of Norman Rockwell's famous "Four Freedoms" paintings.
Moved by Roosevelt's call for Americans to secure the "four essential human freedoms . . . everywhere in the world," and seeking a
way to give a broader and more visceral appeal to these noble but
abstract ideals, the famous illustrator turned to his Vermont neighbors for inspiration. Scenes of day-to-day American life have thus
come to immortalize Roosevelt's internationalist vision: a man
standing up in a town meeting to express an unpopular opinion
stands for freedom of speech; a group of worshippers profiled un-

der the heading "each according to the dictates of his own conscience" represent freedom of worship; a Thanksgiving dinner
evokes freedom from want; finally, a mother and father looking in
on their sleeping children during the London blitz illustrates freedom from fear. Published in four consecutive issues of *The Saturday Evening Post* in February and March 1943, and reproduced as
posters to promote the sale of war bonds that summer, Rockwell's
images were widely distributed. As Westbrook correctly states, the
message that these pictures conveyed was, "with one notable exception [the town meeting scene] . . . , that Americans were fighting World War II to discharge essentially private obligations. And
two of the four paintings conveyed the message that the people of
the United States were fighting for the family."[12] That Americans
were fighting to protect their loved ones, or their cherished way of
life, was, he maintains, "one of the most significant features of
American propaganda during World War II."[13]

In his next essay, the author turns to a less conventional topic:
the pinups of Betty Grable, Rita Hayworth, and other Hollywood
stars that "were all over our ship," as then presidential candidate
and former navy pilot George H. W. Bush admitted in 1988. Like
the photograph of one's real-life sweetheart (sometimes in a pinup
pose) kept in a soldier's wallet, or the name of one's girlfriend
painted on the nose of a plane, these represent for Westbrook further evidence of the American "problem of political obligation."
Without discarding the obvious explanation for the popularity of
pinups, which "functioned as surrogate sex objects for soldiers far
from home,"[14] or neglecting the more immediate problem posed
by the representation of women as objects of protection, Westbrook is more interested in what they reveal of men's reasons to
fight—as he puts it, of the "living theory" of obligation prevalent
at the time. His concern with proving Hobbes true is again illustrated in his conclusion about Grable, who "provided the superior
image of American womanhood" that men fought to protect—or,

more conceptually put, who served to "remove the obfuscating veil of arguments for a soldier's obligation to die for the liberal state [and] to reveal (nakedly) the private obligations upon which such states ultimately relied."[15]

Readers interested in political theory will find Westbrook a joy to read, as I do. The argument is intellectually stimulating, and it does reveal important aspects of American culture. The examples provided to illustrate the appeal to private obligations are convincing. But does his work effectively show that this theme represented "the centerpiece" of wartime propaganda and, by extension, of Americans' "felt obligation"? The author does give some consideration to counterevidence, namely, to the existence of other ideological currents that could have been used to shape wartime obligation—and in so doing, he evokes Rogers Smith's multiple tradition thesis[16] and John Bodnar's characterization of patriotic thought as "a maze." As these authors have suggested, American political culture has been shaped by multiple traditions, including liberalism and republicanism, not just one.[17] But Westbrook considers these alternative messages only to dismiss them as marginal to the mainstream liberal discourse, which remained, in his view, hegemonic.[18]

Westbrook's analysis of counterexamples seems reasonably convincing, such as his treatment of Americans' "grudging admiration" or "lament" for the type of collective purpose embraced by their Japanese enemy.[19] This is illustrated in a Birds Eye Foods advertisement that merged national and familial symbols by portraying Uncle Sam sitting at the head of a Thanksgiving dinner table.[20] Such similarity with what Americans perceived to be dominant in the Japanese political culture was, argues the author, too controversial to become popular: "Yet this argument was rare because it presented a grave difficulty: It came perilously close to the theories of political obligation advanced by the enemy, particularly the Japanese, who justified dying for the state (the emperor) on the grounds that theirs was (quite literally) a family state."[21] The explanation for the rarity of this message is logical, but, as in other alternative messages considered by the author, we are asked to accept at face value the author's assertion that it was indeed rare.

Another nonliberal image that Westbrook considers and rejects as unrepresentative of the ideological construction of "why we fought" is Rockwell's use in *Freedom of Speech* of the town meeting, which represents "a moment in the politics of a state that some democratic philosophers have contrasted to the liberal state, not as a bodyguard or an insurance company for the private interests of citizens but a political community providing a common life for citizens as citizens." Westbrook dismisses the illustrator's use of this classic American symbol of collective and participatory democracy as exceptional, but he also goes a step further to suggest that "Rockwell's portrait of this political community was . . . unwitting." What had mostly impressed the famous illustrator at the town meeting he had just attended, further explained the author, was that his model, Jim Edgerton, had been "allowed to voice his objections on a proposed policy without being shouted down by his neighbors. It was not political community that Rockwell saw himself celebrating in his painting, but tolerance of individual dissent, the use of free speech to protect private conscience from the state." Hence the collective theme that one could legitimately read in the painting had somehow "eluded Rockwell's intentions . . . principally because he happened to live in a part of the country where a remnant of face-to-face participatory democracy survived, and he placed his dissenter (who is difficult to recognize as such) in the midst of this remnant."[22]

Westbrook's analysis raises issues that are beyond the scope of this essay to address, including Rockwell's intentions and Vermont's anachronism. Most important, however, is the currency that representations of collective identity such as those suggested by *Freedom of Speech* held in American wartime culture. Reading

*Freedom of Speech* as a celebration of individualism or as a depiction of the collective and republican ideal for which the town meeting stands might be a case of seeing the glass as half empty or half full. Regardless of one's interpretation of this particular painting, however, the bigger question remains: Were Americans called to join the war effort—to serve, fight, and possibly die for their country—through appeals to their liberal, individualist, and familial selves, or did wartime propaganda and Americans' "felt obligation" also centrally include references to their collective and civic selves? Westbrook feels strongly that only the former proposition is true. But his essays do not demonstrate that appeals to the collective and national identity of Americans were marginal, as he claims they were. While the evidence that the author presents to illustrate the appeal to private motivations is convincing, the claim that these were *central* to the wartime conception of service and obligation to the state is not sustained, and is perhaps unsustainable given the volume and diversity of images produced during the war. Ultimately, the effort to fit wartime political culture into a Hobbesean framework, as intellectually fascinating as it may be, does violence to the multiplicity of messages and ideological inconsistencies through which Americans were called to risk their lives for, or simply to serve, their country.[23]

*6*

## GENDERED PATRIOTS

A rich literature documents the gendered nature of American citizenship. The work of Linda Kerber, in particular, has shown that the complex balance of rights and obligations that constitutes national citizenship has been applied differently to men and women over the years because of the cultural prescription that a woman's primary obligation is to the family. The family, in this framework, competes with the nation for a woman's first and foremost loyalty. How, then, has this particular combination of calls to public service and gendered constraints manifested itself in the public rhetoric of wartime America? The service of women was actively sought during the war not only as home-front producers and consumers but also in the military. Yet their patriotic contribution was never divorced from their prescribed gender roles. Examining the gendered connotations that permeated the rhetoric of national sacrifice reveals important dynamics of differentiation (and power) at work in wartime society.[1]

As America entered a state of "full employment" in early 1943, segments of the population not regularly gainfully employed had to be drawn into the labor market. Women, and especially white, married middle-class women, who had a marginal rate of prewar

employment, represented a rich source of untapped "manpower."
Many responded to the call, and, as the historian Karen Anderson has summarized, their motivations for doing so were varied:
"Economic necessity, the excitement and challenge of war work,
the need to cope with the loneliness and anxiety caused by having
husbands and sons overseas, a disaffection from housework, a desire for more social independence, the sense of purpose accompanying productive work, and other such personal considerations
complemented the desire to help in the war effort." But the pros-
pect of women entering the labor force in large numbers, and in
occupations formerly reserved for men, such as in heavy industry,
generated tangible cultural fears. Only one-sixth of all women
employed during the war worked in the defense industry, and the
majority of new entries were older women, not mothers of young
children; yet concerns that the emergency would lead to a challenge to the traditional family structure—nurtured by the female
homemaker and mother and economically supported by the male
breadwinner—were considerable.[2]

Defense of home and family constituted a salient part of wartime propaganda. But the "innocent, vulnerable mother . . . who
was depending on soldiers to protect her way of life" coexisted
with "the strong, dependable patriot who could run a machine,"
explains the historian Maureen Honey. The iconic Rosie the Riveter popularized by Norman Rockwell's cover illustration for the
May 19, 1943, *Saturday Evening Post* represented the latter: mus-
cular and patriotic (she steps on a copy of *Mein Kampf*), she exudes
self-confidence, yet the disruptive implications of her adoption of
a masculine role are softened by her retention of feminine characteristics (she is wearing lipstick and rouge). Rosie stood for the
female industrial worker who would help win the war and, hope-
fully, return to her domestic duties afterward. The emphasis placed
in popular culture on the patriotic motivations bringing women
into the labor force made their transgressions of gender roles pal-

atable. In Honey's words, "The progressive idea that women could perform all kinds of work in society was accompanied, however, by a shrill patriotic appeal that undermined its potential as a feminist reordering of national values." One common strategy was to downplay individualistic, materialistic self-interest and ambition and to celebrate, instead, the spirit of self-sacrifice and cooperation. "The war worker, as the most visible manifestation of wartime changes, became a powerful symbol of this collective spirit— national purpose, civilian dedication, and home-front support for soldiers. The emphasis was not on women's right to be treated fairly and judged as individual workers but on their heroic service to the nation, a duty that required self-sacrifice and putting the welfare of soldiers above one's own desires."[3]

The importance of patriotic obligation to contain women's assertion of individual rights can also be traced in the demobilization rhetoric that proclaimed women's primary obligation to the returning veterans, whose sacrifice was considered greater than theirs. Any rights or privileges that women might have accrued through their wartime contribution to the national effort—higher wages and the knowledge that they could perform well beyond their employment ghettos, for instance—were now subordinated to their duty of helping veterans to readjust. As the historian Susan M. Hartmann concludes, "While women were assigned the crucial responsibility for solving this major problem [of veterans' readjustment], they were to do so in terms of traditional female roles. Through self-abnegation, by putting the needs of the veteran first, women might successfully renew their war-broken relationships, but they would do so at the price of their own autonomy."[4]

The complex system of rationing put in place in March 1943 also required women's full commitment. Along with Rosie the Riveter, the Wartime Homemaker was thus a central feature of wartime cultural production. At the end of America's first year at war, rubber, gas, sugar, and coffee had been rationed. But in February and March 1943, an extensive governmental control of supply and prices on canned goods, meats, cheese, fats, and butter was put in place, both to guarantee an adequate supply for American and Allied military personnel and to control inflation. A point system, with different point values assigned to different products with varying implementation and expiration dates, was put in place. Daily newspapers kept consumers informed of critical rationing information:

Tomorrow—*Coffee* coupon No. 25 expires. Last day to use No. 4 "A" coupon, good for four gallons of *gasoline.*

March 22—Coupon No. 26 in Ration Book No. 1 becomes valid for 1 pound of *coffee* until April 25.

March 25—*Processed food* stamps for April, D, E and F in Ration Book No. 2 become valid. The monthly quota of 48 points remains unchanged. Budget these through April 30.

March 31—Last day to use A, B, and C point coupons for processed foods in Ration Book No. 2. Deadline for first *tire inspection* for "A" cards.

April 12—Last day for period 4 *fuel oil* coupons.

June 15—Last day for coupon No. 17 good for one pair of *shoes.*

In order to explain and enforce this complex system, which was at first negatively received, an elaborate public relations campaign was launched. It explained to housewives how to shop according to the point system and encouraged them to modify their cooking habits to produce nutritious meals out of rationed ingredients. Female anthropologists such as Margaret Mead and Ruth Benedict were consulted to identify the best ways to induce women to change their consumption patterns. In addition, an extensive network of mostly female volunteers was recruited to monitor consumers' and merchants' compliance with governmental directives in shops across the country. Thus consumption became regulated in a much more pervasive, and effective, manner than wartime production ever was.[5]

The values and meaning of wartime citizenship that were articulated in the public relations campaigns related to rationing, as in the propaganda created to recruit and constrain Rosie, explicitly asserted a hierarchy of sacrifice. Female consumers were called to do their part for the war effort by curtailing their food consumption in order that fighting men—whose sacrifice, it was explicitly stated, was greater—be accommodated. As a guide produced by the Office of War Information about the rationing program explained, "Nothing in this war is more important than tough and well-equipped fighting men . . . [Therefore,] it is important to emphasize that the requirements of our armed forces must be met *first*." Home-front rationing would work only if consumers accepted the proposition that the service of civilians was less onerous and less important than that of military personnel. In this equation, the (female) civilian was subordinated to the (male) soldier. Thus, one of the key functions of the publicity campaigns designed to promote acceptance of rationing was to "educate" women about their lesser civic worth.[6]

In addition to providing service on the home front, women were called to join the military when on May 15, 1942, Roosevelt signed a bill authorizing the formation of the Women's Auxiliary Army Corps. The incentive to include women formally in the armed forces had come from organized women and female politicians who were determined to reap rewards for their wartime military service. Military leaders, most prominently Chief of Staff General George Marshall, appreciated the advantages to be gained from an influx of women into the armed forces, especially given the composition of the modern military organization, which required extensive support personnel for every combatant (88 percent of army personnel were in noncombat positions during the war). Access to women's occupational skills, traditionally honed in office and service jobs, Marshall recognized, was crucial for his modern army. Indeed, the majority of women who served in the military did so in traditional "women's jobs."[7]

At first, women were invited to volunteer to serve *with*, but not *in*, the army (as "auxiliaries" they were denied the same benefits as male soldiers and officers).[8] After September 1943, when the "auxiliary" status was replaced by full military designation, women in the Corps received all the privileges of military service (including access to the benefits provided by the GI Bill at the end of the war), with one telling exception: unlike male military personnel, they did not have access to dependents' benefits. As explained by Leisa Meyer, cultural prescriptions that military service was a masculine prerogative, and fears that women's military service might upset traditional gender roles, were prominent in the congressional and public controversies that the WAC generated throughout the war. As she discusses in the case of allowances for dependents, these "were crucial to the construction of male soldiers as both protectors and breadwinners. By barring female soldiers from access to these allotments House members revealed their uneasiness with the idea of either female protectors or female breadwinners."[9] Defenders of the bill also reinforced distinctions between "women" and "soldiers" when they insisted that women's service was needed to release men for combat duties (in spite of the fact that the great majority of male soldiers did not engage in combat). Other objections to women's service point to the usual—and inconsistent—portrayal of women's vulnerability and power. In response to these concerns, the WAC, under the leadership of a conservative southern newspaper editor, Oveta Culp Hobby, maintained strict regulation to ensure women's respectability while in the service and emphasized conservative gender roles. Not only did public relations efforts present "female soldiers as feminine in appearance, sexually respectable, and less powerful than their male counterparts,"[10] but themes of patriotic sacrifice and self-lessness dominated Hobby's vision of female military service.

Although patriotic sacrifice was present in public discussion of women's military service, and especially prevalent in the views of its conservative leaders, conflicting assertions of women's self-interest and autonomy were also recruiting tools used to attract women into the WAC. Interestingly, Meyer describes the tension that existed between the WAC director's vision of women's self-sacrifice—their military service, she believed, should be a selfless act—and the reality that women were attracted to the Corps for less noble reasons. Young and Rubicam, the prestigious public relations firm retained to advise WAC recruiters in March 1943, noted the discrepancy: the WAC should move away from the "old unsuccessful idea that it's a girl's patriotic duty to join," reported the advertising experts. They pressed for a greater emphasis on the more "glamorous" aspects of military service, such as the "opportunities for training, new skills, education, travel, and adventure women would find in the service." In the end, a compromise was reached by which both sacrifice and personal gain were included in the recruitment material: "I joined to serve my country . . . and I'm having the time of my life!" proclaimed an attractive young white woman in uniform.[11]

Women did not venture into the world of patriotic sacrifice with impunity. A careful cultural production was deployed to contain the potential disruptions to the social order that their real-time war contribution represented. That cultural production illustrates the gendered nature of obligations, and the malleability of wartime rhetoric.

# COMMENTARY
## by Robert D. Johnston

Take a look at the maniacal figure in the "Pour it on!" poster in chapter 4. A close, careful look. The great promise of using a visual source in a history book is that it has such power, such immediacy. But in our overstimulated and intensely visual culture, a significant problem is that we simply glance at a photo, perhaps recognize the creativity of an artwork, and then move far too quickly back to the main story in the written part of the text (if our eyes and brain don't ignore the text altogether in order to proceed to the next fleeting image).

The result: we don't slow down enough to appreciate how difficult it is to critically explore these visual texts—or how important such a task is. Fortunately, Murray's fourth chapter is a model for how to display such visual sources in the context of a gentle but important set of interpretive points.

Of course, the interpretive point that matters most in part II is Murray's disagreement with Robert Westbrook in chapter 5. Murray is at the height of her intellectual bravery here, if only because Westbrook is renowned as one of our most important American cultural and intellectual historians. Yet Murray has no trouble disagreeing with Westbrook. We should not take such disagreement for granted; in some ways, it is amazing that any historian can read carefully, think intelligently, and then make her own claim against an established authority. That's part of the openness and democracy of historical dialogue, where supposed expertise and status don't mean anything if you haven't connected your sources to a compelling analysis, or if you haven't thought creatively and imaginatively.

That openness—that democracy of dialogue—includes students. I therefore urge you to insert yourself into the dispute between Murray and Westbrook. Murray herself welcomes you to this conversation, even inviting disagreement with her as she states, "Some readers may be inclined to side with Westbrook's conclusions instead of my own."

Honestly, I'm still trying to figure out my own preference here, because the arguments on both sides are so good. That's one of the signs of a rich, robust interpretive disagreement. No one has to win, as readers turn the questions raised over and over in their heads.

But I find myself leaning toward Westbrook. I'll admit to being somewhat seduced by his subject matter—the political theory of his father's pinup posters!—as well as by the elegance of his interpretation. Murray notes that Westbrook's essays are "a joy to read," and she's quite right. Yet I hope that it is the intellectual power of Westbrook's arguments that most wins me over. Westbrook starts with a critically important premise—that the political culture of the modern United States is monolithically "liberal." "Liberal" here doesn't mean Democratic Party liberal, but rather liberal in the sense of classical political philosophy, in that our country has no imposing traditional authority, no cohesive community, no mystical fatherland that can command the spontaneous allegiance of autonomous individuals. That's a real problem when it comes to fighting a war—a time when the government must persuade millions of citizens to put their lives on the line. As a result, the government has to appeal to essentially private interests—defending the family around the Thanksgiving dinner table, or protecting your leggy sweetheart—in order to induce men to give to their country their last full measure of devotion.

With this argument, Westbrook has offered a terribly important insight into our nation's history. In many ways we have been—and are—a nation of supreme individualists, and Westbrook uses this analysis to offer a compelling and original way of exploring the underlying political meanings of the visual artifacts of World War II.

But wait, Murray says! Westbrook is claiming that such appeals to private interest were, with very few exceptions (such as Norman Rockwell's *Freedom of Speech* painting), the *only* way the government tried to claim the allegiance of its wartime citizenry. Yet she argues that Westbrook never demonstrates in any systematic way that appeals to public interest were rare—a task seemingly necessary to the success of his argument. Murray comes out of a tradition that recognizes several different kinds of political theory in our country's history—not just Westbrook's individualist liberalism, but also, for example, hierarchical authoritarianism, inegalitarian racism, and small-scale communitarianism—so she suspects that Westbrook is generalizing too much. There has to be more complexity—and the burden is on Westbrook to prove otherwise.

I am attracted to Murray's message here, despite my general preference for scholars who issue sharp, bold, controversial, and challenging provocations. The famous historian J. H. Hexter called this kind of historian a "lumper," because such a scholar lumps together wide and disparate sources into an elegant, unified interpretation (sometimes at the expense of ignoring contrary evidence). The opposite of the "lumper" is the "splitter"—the scholar who appreciates complexity and who takes wide and disparate sources and fashions from them a broad and diffuse interpretation (sometimes at the expense of failing to bring much coherence or general meaning to the story of the past).[1]

Why are some scholars lumpers and some splitters? Personality, perhaps—certain folks can live with a messy living room, and perhaps those people can also live with a messy sense of history. Again, though, the answer may flow in significant ways from politics. And as with Eric Foner in part I, Murray again neglects to unravel this thread. In this case, Westbrook comes out of a tradition of radical populist democracy that celebrates the people's wisdom but sees advocates of genuine democracy in American history as few and far between. Westbrook is therefore something of a prophet crying in the wilderness, trying to convince competitive, individualist Americans that they need to turn toward their public obligations lest the nation perish. Prophets, however, are known for their strenuous moral exhortation—not for their complexity.

Murray herself is clearly also democratic in instinct and historical practice. She cares deeply about ordinary people and believes them to be, in general, thoughtful and ethical. She is also quite concerned about the many obstacles to democracy in our nation's history. Yet she seems fundamentally different from Westbrook in seeing the forces of democracy, goodwill, and community as fairly evenly matched against those of oppression, selfishness, and rampant individualism. Historical interpretation is, in the end, just as much about "historians' own intellectual journeys" and temperament as it is about a simple "immersion in [the] historical record." So the lesson here is to make history personal. Start exploring the ways in which your temperament, and your politics, influence the ways you interpret the past.

After her vigorous intellectual disputation with Westbrook, I have to admit that I am a bit disappointed in Murray's "fairly conventional type of historical writing" in the part's final chapter. Her goal is to demonstrate how, through a careful reading of historical scholarship, we can distill valuable themes—in this case, that American women were not allowed to be patriotic outside the gender roles that confined them and kept them dependent and second-class citizens. Yet despite the importance of this issue, no historical controversy or disagreement intrudes—except in a lonely and buried endnote in which she mentions a disagreement between the historians Amy Bentley and Meg Jacobs. (Note to readers who do relish scholarly argumentation: be sure to look in the endnotes!)

Murray's genius lies in seeing, and practicing, historical pluralism. Here, though, she presents just one story. I urge you to think of, and research, others.

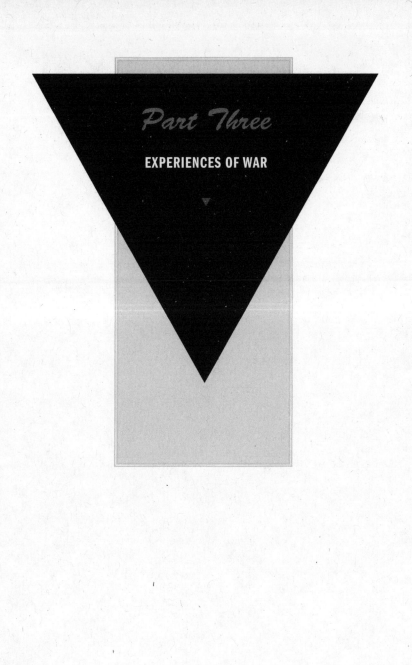

## Part Three

## EXPERIENCES OF WAR

▼

Whether they were mobilized for military service or civilian contribution to the war effort, individuals saw their day-to-day lives profoundly disrupted. The experience of war was especially disruptive—even traumatic—for combatants. The small minority of service personnel who actually saw the front lines found themselves in what the historian Gerald Linderman has called a "world within war": a universe that was, and continues to be, unintelligible to the noncombatant. How, then, did they relate to the national community—to "folks back home"? Chapter 7 attempts to answer this question through an analysis of the journalist Ernie Pyle's dispatches, which, like Roosevelt's public speeches and the propaganda posters, constitute a readily available body of primary sources. Pyle's words mediated the experience of combatants for a domestic audience—they did not, could not, exactly relate it. The essay's central argument about the ultimate incommunicability of the combatants' reality is a result, partly, of the journalist's own marginal role in the "world within war." This is a case in which the choice of sources directly shaped the argument crafted by the historian—had the essay instead analyzed combatants' memoirs, no doubt other themes and an alternative thesis would have emerged.

Chapter 8 explores the experiences of conscientious objectors and Americans of Japanese descent—two groups that were peculiarly confronted with an affront to their patriotic loyalty—through an extended review essay. The books reviewed are published collections of personal letters, which provide anchorage points from which to offer a reflection, rather than an argument, on how these individuals negotiated the particularly painful negation of their national identity.

Chapter 9 considers the broader issue of racial and cultural minorities' place in the nation through a topical essay, similar to the one presented on the gendered definitions of patriotic sacrifice. Here the experiences of Jewish Americans, Native Americans, and African Americans are discussed, and historical interpretations are offered on their integration, or marginalization, in the American political community.

All the groups considered here—frontline combatants, conscientious objectors, and racial and cultural minorities—were marginal in the population at large: statistically, they represented a small minority of the population, and they held little power. Yet their war experiences help us better understand American national identity. As is often the case, it is by looking in from the outside that we see more clearly a society's values.

# 7

From a population of 132 million Americans, 16.3 million persons served in the U.S. military between 1940 and 1946, and fewer than 1 million saw direct fire. Although a minority among servicemen, combat soldiers occupied a special place in the hearts and minds of folks back home. Not only did a large number of American families have a son, brother, husband, sweetheart, or father at the front, but, as stressed in one publicity campaign after another, the "boys" were the ones risking their lives for the patriotic cause. Both personal bonds of affection and official propaganda kept them close to home. Yet, as some historians have argued, the combat soldier himself existed in a world of his own, far removed from family and nation. The reality of combat, wrote Gerald Linderman, "imposed on soldiers a drastically altered existence"—a "world within war." Not only was the experience of combat unique and traumatic, but it was incommunicable. "The real war," observed Walt Whitman famously during the Civil War, "will never get in the books."[1]

War correspondents were among those who attempted to translate the experience of combat to the folks behind the front and back home. During World War II, more than sixteen hundred

American journalists, photographers, and cartoonists were ac-
credited to the various branches of the armed forces. As described
by the Associated Press journalist Don Whitehead, while many
reporters wrote "what are known to the trade as 'colorful' and
'gripping' battle stories from maps, briefings and handouts" distributed by the public relations office at the rear, some joined the
men at the front to tell readers "what war was really like": their
firsthand experience of combat in a foxhole with the infantry, on a
bomber flying over Germany, on a ship in the Pacific, or on an island with the marines led to some of the best of World War II reporting. They left evocative testimonies of the reality of war. But
did they, could they, convey its full meaning? Could they bridge
the gulf that separated families and nation from their loved ones?
Like the censored letters that soldiers sent home or the combat
memories that remained largely unshared after the end of the war,
combat reportage offered a tenuous link between the world within
war and the rest of wartime America.[2]

The literature by war correspondents is, of course, vast. The novelist John Steinbeck was one who joined the ranks of reporters
and filed dispatches for the *New York Herald Tribune* in 1943. In
his account of the landing at Salerno, Italy, for instance, he described men as cogs, "bolts," in the machine of modern warfare:
"Modern warfare is very like an automobile assembly line. If one
bolt in the whole machine is out of place or not available, the line
must stop and wait for it." Alternatively, he compared men to ants
who "crawled on the ships" or crabs who "scuttl[ed] . . . from bits
of cover to other cover" on the beach. They are anonymous soldiers without individuality and without memory—they "disap-
pear into the blackness and the silence" and "do not remember"
battle. "Perhaps all experience which is beyond bearing is that
way. The system provides the shield and then removes the mem-

ory, so that a woman can have another child and a man can go into combat again."[3]

In contrast with Steinbeck's impersonal descriptions of modern war, other reporters such as Ernie Pyle and Don Whitehead gave names and faces to men in the infantry, and they sought to describe the war from their perspectives. Pyle, who lived with the infantry in North Africa and Europe for extended periods between 1943 and 1945, was the most famous among several accomplished combat correspondents. When he was killed by enemy fire on a small island near Okinawa, on April 18, 1945, his popularity among combatants and civilians alike was unmatched. As his biographer James Tobin described, as soon as the reporter arrived in London on his first overseas assignment in December 1940, he was captivated by the day-to-day experience of war. Much as the radio broadcaster Edward R. Murrow had done since the beginning of the German bombing of the English countryside in August, and then of London in September, Pyle wanted to make "people at home see what I see." Unlike Murrow, who clearly sided with the interventionists to urge American involvement in the European war in 1940, Pyle was "tone-deaf to high politics, even to the point of uncertainty whether England was wholly in the right and Germany wholly wrong. What he sought was the personal experience of war. He was eager to immerse himself in its sights and sounds." His attraction to wartime Europe was experiential, not ideological.[4]

Pyle's coverage of the American troops training in Ireland and England in the late summer of 1942 continued in the style that had characterized his Depression-era reporting and would become his trademark. He wrote about the kind of "low-altitude stuff" that pleased his editor at the Scripps-Howard newspaper chain: "Folks with 'boys' over there are a damned sight more interested in reading the homely, every day, what do they eat and how do they live sort of stuff, than they are in reading the heavy strategic, as-I-predicted-in-my-analysis-back-in-1920 sort of stuff."[5] The popularity of Pyle's columns, which increased after he arrived in North Africa in November 1942, seemed to prove the editor right. By April 1943, more than one hundred newspapers published his column, with a combined circulation estimated at nearly nine million.[6]

Pyle's dispatches featured decent, hardworking Americans who cared little for ideological or patriotic sentimentality. They were "the God-damned infantry," as he famously called them on May 2, 1943—"just guys from Broadway and Main Street" who did what they had to do: "Men at the front suffering and wishing they were somewhere else, men in routine jobs just behind the lines belly-aching because they can't get to the front, all of them desperately hungry for somebody to talk to besides themselves."[7] As Tobin put it, Pyle's prototypical hero was the "suffering servant."[8] In Pyle's words, "They are the mud-rain-frost-and-wind boys. They have no comforts, and they even learn to live without the necessities. And in the end they are the guys that wars can't be won without."[9] Like Willie and Joe, the "unshaven, unwashed, unsmiling" characters of Bill Mauldin's cartoons, Pyle's heroes were the ordinary soldiers who lived through the monotony and discomfort of life at the front and endured the horror of battle.[10]

The reporter established a close rapport with both GIs and their families. Infantrymen respected the older journalist (at forty-two, in 1942, Pyle was more than twenty years older than the average GI). He visited their tents and foxholes, struck up conversations in a casual, nonintrusive way, and described their world with empathy. Families eager to connect with "their boys" on the front devoured Pyle's column and wrote to him personally. One woman from New York asked: "Would you Be So Kind to Look up my Boy and Let us know in your paper How He is getting along." As Tobin describes, "the bond between Pyle and his readers was far more intimate [than was customary between a reporter and his readers]. Strangers sent him family photos, clippings, drawings, life

histories. They offered him home remedies. They shipped pack-
ages of soap, books and cookies ... One letter writer in three begged
Ernie to look up a particular soldier, either just to say hello or to
check on his safety or to find out why he had not written a letter
home in so long."[11] He was, according to one commentator, "the
only war correspondent to become a legend in his own lifetime."[12]

Don Whitehead, a reporter for the Associated Press, left Man-
hattan for Cairo in the fall of 1942. Like Pyle, he proudly counted
himself among an elite group of combat correspondents. The diary he kept at the time illustrates his thrill at having been chosen
for the job: "It seemed slightly absurd to be writing of movie stars,
Harlem and front page celebrities when there was a war to write
about—the raw material of death and agony and heroism."[13] After
a stint with the First Infantry Division in North Africa, he joined
the invasion forces in the Sicilian, Italian, and Normandy landings (thus earning the nickname of "Beachhead Don"). He then
followed the troops through France and Belgium and into Germany. His dispatches, like Pyle's, reveal the experience of war in
rich detail—the movements, the sounds, the smells, and the sights
of battle. They are framed in the first person singular, which, along
with firsthand observations, adds immediacy and veracity to his
descriptions: "I dodged into a slit trench as the first bomb whis-
tled down. The ear-splitting crash made the earth shudder. Smoke,
dirt and the acrid fumes of burnt powder rolled over." As he reminded his readers: "I was lucky enough to be on the scene for the
two most crucial battles of the Sicilian campaign, and so I was not
only able to get observations of men on the scene, but I watched
the battle from close range and was in position to draw my own
conclusions." Like Pyle, Whitehead not only celebrated the foot
soldiers but also personalized them by including their names and
hometowns in his stories: "This battalion, under Maj. Charles
(Chuck) Horner, Doylestown, Pa., was to drive straight to Troina ...

Below us in the wheat stubble Pvt. Christopher Finley, High Splint, Ky., and Sgt. Benjamin Fiarowich of New York City, are sweeping for mines."[14]

While sharing key features, Pyle's and Whitehead's World War II reports differ in one key respect. Pyle's writing reflects an explicit awareness that, as crucial as it was to convey to audiences back home the combatant's experience of war, the task was ultimately impossible. Near the end of the war, Pyle confessed to General Dwight Eisenhower that the ideal of "making people see what I see" was futile. "War, the extreme human experience, tests the limits of human communication."[15] His heart-to-heart exchange with Eisenhower was not unusual for Pyle. In fact, on a regular basis in his column, he held much the same conversation with the American public. Pyle, like other combat correspondents, saw himself as a mediator between frontline soldiers and the rest of the nation; yet, in contrast with most, including Whitehead, he constantly reminded his readers that they would never—could never— understand the experience of combat. As much as Pyle embodied a desire for connection between the front and home, the impossibility of explaining the inexplicable constituted a dominant theme of his wartime writing. This clear theme in Pyle's message to the American people, which makes him, one could say, the Walt Whitman of the twentieth century, is worth examining more closely.


On November 10, 1942, two days after American troops landed in Morocco and Algeria, Pyle left Britain in a convoy that reached Oran on November 23. After a stint with the air force at Biskra, Algeria, he joined the army's II Corps in central Tunisia in February 1943. It was there that he immersed himself for the first time in frontline life.[16] As his biographer described it: "Ernie had always been the outsider with people he covered, the casual observer alighting briefly, then moving on." Now, with the army, he was possessed, as he himself wrote, by a "feeling of vitality, of being in the heart of everything, of being a part of it—no mere onlooker, but a member of the team." In early April, after returning to Algiers, he reflected that he "resented dropping out even long enough to do what I was there to do—which was write. I would rather have just kept going all day, every day."[17]

The difference between the combat soldier and "the rest of us" was captured in his "Brave Men, Brave Men!" dispatch of April 22, 1943. He was then returning to his "old friends at the front," and he noticed the transformation they had undergone through their recent combat experience. This column is memorable for Pyle's commentary on the soldiers' newly acquired outlook on killing: "The most vivid change is the casual and workshop manner in which they now talk about killing. They have made the psychological transition from the normal belief that taking human life is sinful, over to a new professional outlook where killing is a craft." Especially in light of the realization that his friends had become professional killers, he again reflected on the gap that separated noncombatants—"all the rest of us," including himself—from combat soldiers:

> I think I am so impressed by this new attitude because it hasn't been necessary for me to make this change along with them. As a noncombatant, my own life is in danger only by occasional chance or circumstance. Consequently I need not think of killing in personal terms, and killing to me is still murder . . .
>
> In this one respect the front-line soldier differs from all the rest of us. All the rest of us—you and me and even the thousands of soldiers behind the lines in Africa—we want terribly yet only academically for the war to get over. The front-line soldier wants it to be got over by the physical process of his destroying enough Germans to end it. He is truly at war. The rest of us, no matter how hard we work, are not.[18]

Occasionally, as in his famous column of May 2, 1943 ("The God-Damned Infantry"), written shortly after he had advanced into combat with the troops under constant shelling for four days, he included himself as one of them: "my division," "our ridge," "our battalion." Yet he never ceased feeling "like a spectator instead of a participant . . . which is, of course, all that a correspondent is or ever should be."[19] When he left Italy in early May 1944, in reporting his mixed feelings about leaving the front, he again revealed his ambivalence about his status: "I've been in this war theatre so long that I think of myself as a part of it. I'm not in the Army, but I feel sort of like a deserter at leaving." His public farewell to his pals was emotional and confused:

> To all . . . of you in this Mediterranean army of ours—it has been wonderful in a grim, homesick, miserable sort of way to have been with you . . .
>
> I've hated the whole damn business just as much as you do who have suffered more. I often wonder why I'm here at all, since I don't have to be, but I've found no answer anywhere short of insanity, so I've quit thinking about it. But I'm glad to have been here.[20]

Regardless of how long he spent with the infantry, how deeply he felt for their plight, or how tangibly he described their experience, ultimately Pyle remained a correspondent—an intermediary between the troops and the folks back home. He had the liberty to choose whether he would stay at the front.

Just as Pyle alternated in how he described his relation to the troops, he projected to his readers his ambivalence between his conviction that they should know about life at the front and his realization that, no matter how hard he or they tried, they never would know. This inherent contradiction of modern war was expressed through his direct admonitions to his readers—another aspect of Pyle's writing that distinguished him from other combat correspondents.

Don Whitehead also admonished his readers, but he did so in the third person—through the soldiers whose experiences and feelings his dispatches conveyed. Writing from Italy on November 23, 1943, Whitehead described "a red-haired kid from Vermont reading a letter from home. His boots were two balls of mud and his clothes were soaked." His unit had been fighting through mountains for thirty days. "The kid sighed and thoughtfully folded the letter and slipped it carefully into a wallet. 'The folks back home do not quite know what we are up against, do they,' he said. 'It looks like they think we are having a picnic and that it's all over but the shouting. I wish they could see for themselves what it is like out here.'" Another instance in which Whitehead addressed domestic audiences, again indirectly, was in June 1944 as the troops were beginning their long trek through occupied France. After the successful Normandy landing, American public opinion had become overly confident that the war was all but won. Whitehead used his pen to dispel this misplaced optimism, but he did so with his typical restraint, speaking through the troops rather than directly to the reader as Pyle did so bluntly, reporting, "Everywhere I find the troops afraid that the people at home are too optimistic."[21]

In contrast, Pyle addressed his audience personally: "It must be hard for you folks at home to conceive how our troops right at the front actually live. In fact it is hard to describe it to you even when I'm among them, living in somewhat the same way they are." He proceeded to describe in several paragraphs "a type of living that is only slightly above the caveman stage." As became constant in his writing, he turned directly to his audience—"You can't conceive how hard it was to move and fight at night"—and described the combat experience while reminding his readers that the experience was beyond their comprehension: "The men lived in a way that is inconceivable to anyone who hasn't experienced it," and "You don't know—can never know, without experiencing it—the awful feeling of being shot at by speeding enemy planes."[22] His famous salute to "the mud-rain-frost-and-wind boys" included an explicit comment to the folks back home: "I wish you could have seen just one of the unforgettable sights I saw." Again, on August 15, 1943, in "One Dull, Dead Pattern Somewhere in Sicily," the journalist described "the terrible weariness that gradually comes over everybody" and reiterated what had become by then a familiar litany: "incomprehensible to you folks back home," "inconceivable to you in the States." A year later he was still writing, with a touch of irony and condescension this time: "For five days and nights . . . I stayed at the front with our troops. And now . . . I want to tell you about it in detail from day to day, if you will be that patient." [23]

In the very last piece he penned before his death in April 1945, he wrote eloquently in anticipation of the victory in Europe. A rough draft of a column he had been preparing for the occasion was found on his body. His feelings of kinship for his friends on the European front were as strong as his mistrust of the folks back home:

Dead men by mass production—in one country after another—month after month and year after year. Dead men in winter and dead men in summer.

Dead men in such familiar promiscuity that they become monotonous.

Dead men in such monstrous infinity that you come almost to hate them.

These are the things that you at home need not even try to understand. To you at home they are columns of figures, or he is a near one who went away and just didn't come back. You didn't see him lying so grotesque and pasty beside the gravel road in France.

We saw him, saw him by the multiple thousands. That's the difference . . .[24]

Better than most other combat correspondents, Ernie Pyle captured in his columns not only the daily experience of combat but also the impossibility of conveying that experience to the non-combatant. The knowledge of that impossibility was never overwhelming, for as tortured as Pyle was, he never stopped writing for a home-front audience. Like his audience, Pyle yearned for a connection that he never achieved.

## *8*

**WRITING HOME: INTIMATE CONVERSATIONS ABOUT WAR**

On February 19, 1942, President Franklin Delano Roosevelt signed Executive Order 9066, authorizing military authorities to remove the entire population of Japanese descent from the west coast of the United States. About 120,000 people were taken from their homes in the spring and early summer. They were sent at first to assembly centers made of hastily converted county fairgrounds and racetrack stables, then relocated under armed guard to concentration camps in the interior. Not only were Japanese American citizens interned along with their noncitizen parents, but Japanese members of the U.S. Army at the time of the attack on Pearl Harbor—a total of five thousand from the mainland and Hawaii—were reclassified as "aliens not acceptable to the armed forces," reassigned to menial labor, and stripped of their weapons. Internees were understandably astonished when, in early 1943, a call was issued for Japanese American (Nisei) men to volunteer for the United States armed forces in a segregated unit, the 442nd Regimental Combat Team. As Minoru Masuda recalled in the 1970s,

the announcement that the army would be recruiting from the camp . . . fell like a clap of thunder on incredulous ears. How

could the government and the army, after branding us disloyal,
after stripping us of our possessions and dignity, and imprison-
ing us in barbed wire concentration camps, how could they now
ask us to volunteer our lives in defense of a country that had so
wrongfully treated us?[1]

Masuda, nevertheless, was among the 5 percent of mainland Japanese American men of draft age—approximately twelve hundred
in number—who responded to the call in the hope of regaining
their lost citizenship. The draft for Nisei was reinstated in January
1944, after it became clear that volunteers would not be sufficient
to staff the 442nd. By the end of the war, of the 36,000 eligible
Japanese Americans, approximately 20,000 had served in the U.S.
military. A few hundred men openly resisted the draft and were
moved from camps to federal prisons.[2]

Minoru Masuda was born in downtown Seattle in 1915, where
his parents ran a small hotel. The third of five children, Minoru
earned a master's degree in pharmacology from the University of
Washington in 1938 and married Hana Koriyama in May 1939.
Three years later, in the wake of Pearl Harbor, the couple spent a
summer in "Camp Harmony," the Puyallup Assembly Center south
of Seattle, after which they were relocated to Camp Minidoka near
Hunt, Idaho. "We were assigned to Block 16, Barrack 5, Unit F at
one end of a long tar-paper barrack," recalled Masuda in the 1970s.
"We didn't even have a place to sit down and cry, except the floor."
During their stay in Camp Minidoka, they both worked in the
camp hospital, and in the fall they went to pick potatoes for a Mennonite family in Hunt, with whom they also lived. "It was a very
enjoyable stay away from camp," remembered Masuda.[3] After he
joined the army in 1943, he trained at Camp Shelby in Mississippi
and was shipped overseas in April 1944, where he served as a
medic in Italy and France. He returned home, at first to Minneapolis, Minnesota, where Hana had resettled, then to Seattle in

early January 1946. His parents had left Camp Minidoka only a few months earlier, also resettling once again in the Seattle area.

While the Masudas were at Camp Harmony, in July 1942, Frank Dietrich, a social worker from Pittsburgh, of mixed German American and British parentage, was called to present himself for induction. He was assigned to the Army Air Forces and trained as a radio operator and technician. He taught radio and electronics in stateside training schools before being transferred to the Philippines in May 1945, three months after the Allies liberated Manila. Dietrich was stationed around Manila until his return to San Francisco in December 1945. He was honorably discharged in January 1946 and resettled in Pittsburgh.

Frank's twin brother, Albert, chose a different path. After graduating with a master's degree in social work in June 1941 (a degree Frank had also earned), he took a job in Nebraska, where he lived with a pacifist Mennonite family and joined the Fellowship of Reconciliation (FOR), the nation's largest radical pacifist organization. Exercising the right granted by the 1940 Selective Training and Service Act to exemption from combat duty on the grounds of religious objection, during World War II some twenty-five thousand conscientious objectors (COs) were classified as I-A-O and served in noncombat positions in the military, mostly as medics. Another twelve thousand, including Albert Dietrich, claimed IV-E status, a classification that exempted them from military service but required that they be available for what the Act described rather vaguely as "work of national importance." After induction, those so designated were housed in Civilian Public Service (CPS) camps, most of which were run by the Brethren, Mennonite, and Quaker churches—the three "historic peace churches," so called for their theological opposition to war. A minority of those who rejected military service also refused to subject themselves to the draft or, having failed to convince the draft board of the sincerity of their claims, refused both military or alternative service; these "absolutists," six thousand in total, served prison terms.[4] Albert Dietrich took the middle course and applied for IV-E status in February 1942. When he received his draft registration in June, he was disappointed to learn that he had instead been classified as available for military service (I-A). He promptly filed an appeal, however, which was granted in September 1943, and in early November Dietrich reported for civilian service. He was released from CPS thirty-three months later, in August 1946, a year after the end of the war.

While away in the service, Minoru Masuda wrote almost daily to his wife, Hana. Likewise, the Dietrich brothers kept up a regular correspondence with each other between 1939 and 1946, and Frank wrote extensively to his wife, Christine, as well. Respectively published in *Letters from the 442nd* and *Army GI, Pacifist CO*, these private exchanges offer a valuable addition to an already extensive scholarship on the experience of Japanese Americans and conscientious objectors during World War II. The two books, which present first-person accounts of vastly different war experiences, complement each other well. The tone of the Dietrich brothers' conversations, at times brutally honest, contrasts with Minoru Masuda's muted commentary on issues of war, race, and citizenship. Both are suggestive of the different ways that individuals who were confronted with issues of patriotic loyalty—the Dietrichs in response to Albert's refusal to fight, and Masuda because of his race—experienced their service to the nation. Perhaps most fascinating, however, and probably the chief virtue of these published sets of correspondence, is what they reveal of the place that letter writing itself occupied in these individuals' struggles to make sense of their wartime experiences.[5]

Scott H. Bennett, author of a study of the War Resisters League (an influential secular pacifist organization),[6] offers an important contribution to the field as the editor of *Army GI, Pacifist CO*, a collection of the letters Frank Dietrich exchanged with his brother,

Albert, and wife, Christine. Of the more than 560 letters in the Dietrich correspondence, 170 are reproduced in this volume. Bennett's substantial introduction to the letters highlights the major themes that their correspondence addresses and provides biographical information about the twin brothers. The latter is especially useful in helping the reader to appreciate the transformative impact of their wartime experiences. We learn, for instance, that the Dietrichs' upbringing in the Protestant "substantial middle class" of Pittsburgh was marked by "a paternalistic, biased attitude toward blacks and immigrants."[7] Both brothers later rejected the cultural racism of their childhood, notes Bennett, a statement that is confirmed by Albert's embrace of FOR's antiracist protests during the war.[8] Other elements of their upbringing exercised a more durable influence, notably the summers spent in the culturally rich setting of Chautauqua, New York. Under the guidance of their mother, the twins developed an appreciation for music, books, and ideas that is evident in their wartime letters. They comment, for instance, on their yearning for stimulating discussions: "[I] often get disgusted with the lack of intellectuality within the organizations," Albert noted of the chapter of FOR he joined in Nebraska. "Well, to me, the purpose of the organization is good, but the intellectual attack at the problem is almost nil."[9] Frank partly credited his assignment to the Army Air Forces— "some degree better than the infantry"—to the cultural affinity he shared with the interviewing army official, "himself . . . a violinist familiar with all the great Beethoven quartets."[10] A certain cultural distance from their peers remains almost tangible, especially in the case of Frank. "Most soldiers hurried to bars for drinks when they got their passes for the first time," he noted. "I and another fellow . . . went directly to a record shop and listened to good music."[11]

The letters are presented chronologically, starting with one from Albert dated November 7, 1939, barely two months after the

German invasion of Poland, in which he described a ceramics class he was taking: "I completed a small statuette entitled 'Poland[.]' It is a heavily robed peasant woman kneeling with her head low and her hands covering her face. Right now, I am making a head portrait which I am calling 'The Face of Fascism.' This is a very beastly but powerful face . . ."[12] In spite of his abhorrence of fascism and the growing likelihood of American belligerence, he remained faithful to his pacifist conviction. "My feelings about war and militarism have not changed one iota in spite of all the propaganda and war hysteria," he wrote on August 9, 1941.[13] The arguments against war that Albert articulated in his letters will be familiar to students of pre-1941 anti-interventionism and of pacifism. They ranged from the biblical injunction against killing—"I accept the Lord's commandment, 'Thou shalt not kill.' Without reservations as to time, place or circumstances," he wrote to his local draft board[14]—to a political criticism of British imperialism and Anglo-American war goals, the destructive impact of war and its futility in resolving world problems, and the violation of civil liberties and civil rights that war entails. Although influenced and supported by Mennonite and Brethren friends he met in Nebraska in 1941 and 1942, Albert's pacifism was an individual decision, not one that was rooted, as in the case of members of the historic peace churches, in a long-standing, communal rejection of war.[15]

A well-developed scholarship has documented the substance and nuances of World War II pacifism and the personal experiences of those who opted for civilian public service. Albert Dietrich's accounts of some of these themes—such as his frustration with the insignificant nature of the work performed and the social ostracism he faced as a CO—thus add a personal perspective to the established literature rather than breaking new ground. Similarly, Frank's descriptions of his experience as a noncombat soldier are valuable, but not original. But this does not take away from the importance of this published collection of letters as a window into the self-questioning that could accompany one's decision to resist, or comply with, military service. "This letter, I can see, is going to clear my own thinking considerably," wrote Frank in January 1942. "I know I'll refute my own arguments occasionally. But bear with me."[16] In early 1943, Albert congratulated his brother on his writing, suggesting that it reflected Frank's clarity of thought: "You write well and clearly. Your letters have been getting better & better and it seems that you have been doing a lot of thinking while in the army."[17] He continued with a confession: "As for myself, I wish I could think things out as clearly as you do. I seem to be unable to really formulate my philosophy intellectually." (He had just experienced a grueling interrogation by the appeal board.) Over the course of this long letter, Albert alternated between reflecting on his own uncertainty—"I should like to take some time discussing the points you brought out in your letter, but I am afraid I cannot clear things up, either for you or for myself"—and asserting his position, yet recognizing the legitimate nature of his brother's disagreement: "You are wrong, Frank," he concluded, "your justification of war is too elaborate to hold water . . . But nonetheless, I respect you for the conclusions you have come to and I don't mean to try to make you think differently necessarily."[18] Their exchange continued to be active and passionate in February 1943: "Your last letters were particularly stimulating and I should like to continue our discussion of our philosophies. Writing helps clarify our thinking."[19] Still, in September 1944, Frank confessed: "This is a mess of a letter, hurriedly written. I hope next time I can sit down and do some thinking with you as I write."[20] They wrote not only to stay in touch with each other—although this was clearly important to them—but to explain to themselves and to each other why they should or should not fight.

The decision each brother made was deeply personal, and it was definitive: not once in their six-year conversation did either express fundamental doubts about the path he had chosen. In spite of their contrary convictions, their relationship was mutually affirming. Frank respected his brother's decision not to fight. He actively supported his appeal process by writing to the appeal board to defend the sincerity of his brother's pacifism, and he encouraged Albert to ignore social misconceptions of the CO's stand, as in March 1944, when he commented on firefighting: "The latter has no significance except [to] allay the fears and prejudices of the vigorous flag wavers who believe the chief reason CO's are CO's is because they fear the hazards of battle. That's true and a lot of nonsense at one and the same time. To hell with people like that."[21] He also explained to their extended family Albert's unconventional choice. "He can't find killing others compatible with Christianity," Frank reported to their aunt and uncle during a visit back home.[22] Yet he fundamentally disagreed with his brother's pacifism and perhaps ultimately never quite fully understood it. His frequent and long letters to his brother are thus an explanation—even a justification—of his own support for war, a challenge to his brother's pacifism, and an attempt—probably unsuccessful in the end—to understand Albert's position. The same can be said of Albert's defense of pacifism and his challenge to Frank's embrace of war. Their exchanges were passionate, the expression of their disagreements at times bold and impatient: "Your letter . . . indicates that you understand so little of the pacifist principles that it is almost pathetic," wrote Albert on January 27, 1942.[23] Frank continued to query: "What would [a pacifist] do if an invader came to his very door, massacred his children and took off with his wife; what would he do? . . . Tell me your answer now. This seems to be the very crux of the problem, and I can't quite figure it out."[24] Albert provided a long answer to this "perennial question asked by everyone who does not know the pacifist way of life" in his next letter.[25] In 1946, the brothers were still trying to understand each other's stand: "Your statement . . . amuses me," wrote Albert about Frank's assumption that he would not seek a job with the Veterans Administration. "I really can't see your thinking at all." Ironically, he went on to explain to his sympathetic GI brother that "we C.O.'s have almost universally found more understanding of our position among soldiers & ex-soldiers than anyplace else."[26] Only once, in the midst of a philosophical discussion on the preservation of civilization in September 1945, did Frank seem to let his disagreement shade into disapproval of his brother's stance: "The best we can do is try and if civilization sinks to oblivion *at least some of us fought for her.*"[27] In spite of moments of tension, their letters illustrate, on the whole, that each was making a genuine attempt to reach a fuller understanding of his own and the other's position in the context of a supportive and loving relationship.

In March 1946, in the midst of a heated exchange with his brother about the role of Christianity in ensuring peace, Albert, who was still in camp at the time, noted that he sometimes shared his brother's letters with a broader audience: "My friends here are as much interested in what you say as I am, for I do share your letter[s] occasionally," he wrote.[28] On a previous occasion, in November 1942, Frank had reported on a conversation he had had about Albert's stand with a noncombatant CO who was in training with him. The Dietrich family was not unique in having one son in the service and one who took a CO stand.[29] And given that twenty-five thousand COs entered the service, it is probable that lively conversations around such ethical dilemmas took place in the barracks. How did soldiers and objectors relate to each other? Were the stimulating conversations exchanged between Frank and Albert exceptional, or might they have taken place more commonly?

Between 1939 and 1946, there were lapses in the brothers' correspondence. In the first letter that Frank wrote, one month after being inducted in July 1942, for instance, he reflected on his relative lack of interest in epistolary exchanges. He suggested, although ambiguously, that his silence reflected the ease with which he was adapting to army life:

I thought when I left home I'd be writing long letters to everyone about the Army, but I discovered I was capable of writing very few letters—most of them directed to Dad. It's hard to explain just why. In the first place, I fell into Army life much easier than I expected so that I was really enjoying it and therefore, did not feel the extreme need to maintain outside contacts. In the second place, I found writing letters made me intellectualize just a little too much and I would begin finding myself not liking the Army.[30]

Was writing, then, a way to preserve a civilian identity? On the one hand, he did not feel the need to write because he felt himself adapting quite well to his new military environment; on the other hand, he expressed a fear that writing might distance him from a life that, after all, he was not at liberty to leave. In his next letter to Albert, two weeks later, Frank suggested that perhaps he was not a good fit, after all, among the barracks crowd, that his formal and cultural education, as well as his political views, distanced him from his fellow soldiers:

The crudity of the majority of the boys is positively appaling [sic] to me. It's the rare few who are sensitive to a few of the finer things that sustain my morale. Yesterday I met two liberals—the first I've come upon since I've been a warrior. I know they're around, but it's hard to find them. Most of the boys in my barracks beef about labor as though labor were the great poisonous snake in the grass.[31]

Frank, the "warrior," would come to adapt to army life. By the time he was transferred to the Philippines in April 1945, and during his stay there until the end of the year, he felt a much closer rapport with his buddies. Even the brass was more tolerable: "Instead of the normal barking, biting first sergeant, we met a gentleman, who introduced himself with a friendly hand shake."[32] During this time, he wrote mostly to his wife, partly because of the weight of that separation, and also because Albert, then in the midst of a period of depression, was keeping to himself. Frank's letters to Christine included descriptions of the destruction of Manila, reports of his encounters with Filipinos he had befriended, and discussions of military and political developments, including reflections on peace and international relations that he would normally have exchanged with his brother. The few letters that he wrote to Albert in this period relayed his "hazy and haphazard impressions" of his new environment and conveyed some thoughts on his postwar plans, but they contained none of the philosophical considerations that dominated other periods.[33] It was only in the fall of 1945 that they resumed a more substantial and regular discussion of issues of war and peace.

It was also common for Albert to comment on how the frequent interruptions of camp life made letter writing difficult. After he entered camp on November 9, 1943, Albert's letters became sparse and lacked the critical engagement of earlier times. In September 1944, he got around to responding to a letter his brother had written in mid-July, but he apparently had difficulty putting his heart into it.[34] Close to one year after entering CPS, looking forward to his first furlough, and feeling his service to be meaningless, Albert felt his morale sink to a low point. On October 3, 1944, obviously writing in haste (he used no capitalization in the first half of the letter), he lamented the break in communication: "I have long wanted to sit down & write you a more thoughtful letter, expounding some of my thinking & rationalizing."[35] Apart from the occasional letter in which they returned to a discussion of war and peace, they resumed a substantial correspondence only when Albert was released from camp in August 1946. Among other issues, they then discussed the delayed discharge of COs from CPS camps and postwar liberalism.

In a postscript to a letter dated February 24, 1943, Frank asked his brother to "preserve the letters and someday we'll put them together to see if they would be worth a publisher."[36] At another time, Albert also revealed his awareness of the importance of their correspondence, expressing his wish to get his hands on some of the old letters. A friend had suggested that his recuperation from a broken leg offered an opportunity to "write something and try to sell it to a magazine."[37] They did not write for a broader public, but their intuition that posterity would find their letters of interest was prescient. Sustained over a period of seven years, this set of correspondence, with its spurts of intense debates and lulls in the conversation, offers a fascinating look into the processes by which these individuals strove to make sense of their war experience.

Similarly, the letters of Minoru Masuda, made available by his wife, Hana Masuda, and Dianne Bridgman, former manager of the Washington State Oral History Program, offer a window into Masuda's two years of service for a nation that denied, and then reclaimed, his patriotic loyalty. Recalling the sharp disagreements among Minidoka internees on whether to volunteer, Minoru Masuda explained in the 1970s that his was a "lonely and personal decision." His letters began after he left camp for training and thus do not shed light on what he characterized as his "soul-searching."[38] News of the whereabouts of family and friends, the towns he visited and the souvenirs he collected while on leave, and descriptions of his work as a medic and of the mundane events of his day-to-day life in the service take up most of the pages, along with descriptions of the reality of combat and reflections on the extensive publicity, and military honors, bestowed upon the Nisei soldiers. Masuda's racial consciousness is also discernible in his writing. Like the Dietrich brothers, who dissected and discussed at great length Albert's principled opposition to war but never once suggested that his position was any less patriotic than Frank's, Masuda revealed no conflicted sense of national belonging. His American nationalism was entirely compatible with a Japanese cultural identity.

Only for a brief period after he joined the service did Masuda address his letters to Camp Minidoka. On Thanksgiving Day 1943, Hana left Minidoka to join him in Hattiesburg, Mississippi, where he was training. In a short introduction to this section of the book, Hana Masuda related this event fondly: "Right away I began to feel more cheerful in Hattiesburg—camp was far away. I felt so free."[39] After her husband was shipped overseas, she resettled in Minneapolis, Minnesota, with other members of her family who were also released from camp, including her mother. Although the editors provide no information on Minoru's family, we gather from the letters that his parents, and perhaps his older brother's and sister's families, stayed in camp for the duration of the war, resettling in the Seattle area in the fall of 1945. Two younger sisters were attending college in Greensboro, North Carolina, in the fall of 1943. Masuda seemed to have maintained minimal contact with his parents while in the service, perhaps because of their lack of ease with written Japanese. On September 4, 1945, he mentioned that "Mom and Pop wrote me in *nihongo* for the first time."[40]

His letters to Hana, which he penned almost daily, were clearly a way for Masuda to stay connected: "Maybe I'll see you again tomorrow," he wrote to close a letter in August 1944. "It's about time that we got together again," read his greeting on another occasion.[41] The letters also reveal the broad network of Japanese American friends who surrounded the Masudas and with whom they stayed in close touch in spite of the disruption of war. These friends ranged from fellow students from the University of Washington to new friends they met in Mississippi, many of them from Hawaii.

Masuda also reported with fondness about hearing from former neighbors from camp. One sent him a publication produced by the Minidoka internees: "Brought back many memories—I hope you have a copy," he told his wife.[42] Close to Christmas, he reported: "A surprise package from the residents of Block 10 came too, with some nice contributions. I sent them a thank you note yesterday."[43] Some friends were in Japan during the war; Masuda was moved to get news of them after the end of the war, in November 1945: "Sono Hoshi was still there, and Tish Matsushima's in a TB sanitarium, and . . . Fred Shimanaka had been killed on Saipan . . . and Tosh Funakoshi was a soldier somewhere in one of the fronts. What a mess life can be and what strange destinies fate deals for us!" he remarked.[44] From these letters we gather that for Masuda, home was to be found among the Japanese diaspora. The further dispersion created by war no doubt accentuated the need to stay connected—to "keep the memories alive," as he put it. When Hana suggested that they stay in Minneapolis after the war, he remarked: "We've enough of our friends around there to come and visit us, so we can keep the memories alive."[45]

While most of the letters describe the ordinary, even pleasant aspects of his stay overseas—the places he visited, the pretty girls, the rolling hills of Italy, the gardens and orchards from which they scavenged food for homemade stews, his enjoyment of the rice and other Japanese food he asked Hana to send—he also shared his impressions of the reality of war. He spoke in euphemistic terms of the gruesome nature of combat. "It's very rugged" is the phrase he used to describe war in the midst of twenty-eight days of intense combat near the Arno River in Italy—the 442nd's baptism by fire. His letter of June 30, 1944, was unusual, not only in its brevity but also in its staccato cadence. Its first half reads:

This must necessarily be short—time is very precious and this is a little God-sent time of rest for us battle-weary troops. Not that the war has stopped—but it's not here now. So it's been some time now since I last wrote—we've seen action now. It's very rugged—I won't bore you with the details. Unimportant, but warfare is tough and Sherman was right and more so. But, we're all okay and doing fine. Don't worry one whit about me. When I get back I'll tell you *all* about it.[46]

In his next letter, on July 3, he again wrote euphemistically: "We're getting along fine. Of course, it has been a little tough. But we're going right along. We eat, sleep, and perform our functions whenever and wherever we can and when the time is available. We've had some casualties, naturally, and we've had business. That's not good, but in war it's no picnic."[47] On July 15, he wrote about the primitive conditions under which they were living:

I sleep practically anywhere, eat under any conditions, and live in a manner to make you shudder . . . I eat with blood on my hands, flies buzzing around my food, and with vomit in my sight—it's a matter of getting used to it, I guess. In a war living is reduced to its essentials, though we try hard to hang on to whatever ideals we had before, at least what we call civilization.[48]

His spirit was being worn out by the long engagement, by the "business" of war. Two days later he confessed, "Although it is a beautiful day here, I don't feel particularly happy for we had some—a few—casualties last night and this morning. You know how I'm always happiest when nobody comes here . . ."[49] By the time the 442nd was transferred to the Vosges Mountains in northeastern France, near the German border, Masuda sounded just like any other embittered combat GI.[50] On October 22, after his return from the front, he wrote Hana a long letter in which he described the evacuation stopover they had set up to treat the men, many of whom were suffering from trench foot:

And to top it off, the Medical Department comes out with some crappy memo about GIs must not sleep with wet shoes and socks. How the hell is the infantry man gonna do that when he's out there day and night in the rain fighting the Jerries and takes his shoes off when he goes to sleep. He has no blanket—he's all soaked anyway—even the socks that he carries are probably all wet and he can't carry an extra pair of shoes around. Some of these guys higher up should come around once in awhile instead of sitting in some soft chair giving good advice. But, that gave us all some sort of amusement, ironic as all hell.[51]

After a brief rest, the 442nd was ordered to rescue a Texas regiment, the 141st, that was stranded on a ridge behind German lines. The casualties they suffered in that week were extraordinary. On November 6, Masuda expressed his despair and his companions' frustration: "If this damn outfit doesn't get relieved pretty soon, there's gonna be nothing left of it. All that we're waiting for is relief. The usual latrine talk permeates the atmosphere about that."[52] A week later he wrote again, on the eve of yet another engagement: "Decimated though we are we still have to go into the lines. Sometimes I wonder if they know what they're doing."[53] Masuda's accounts of the reality of combat were not unusual. Masuda saw himself as a typical GI, and, like many others, he complained about the "usual snafu" of military life, and expressed his impatience with "this senseless conflict" and his resignation that it had to be endured.[54] "Well, if that's the way it is, that's the way it is. But we still don't like war one little bit."[55] When distant from the nightmare of combat, even if only after a short while, he regained his composure: "We've pulled back!—and that's no rumor. We'd sweated it out for days and it's actually come to pass . . . If you can only comprehend what that means—to pull back out of the lines. Away from all the things that make war the nightmare that it can be. But now that that's in the past, we may as well enjoy the present to the full and be optimistic about the future."[56]

While on some level his experience was that of any other combat GI, his particular experience as a Japanese American serving in a segregated unit gives Masuda's letters additional significance. He identified as an American, proudly so at times. "I was quite proud when they played our anthem," he wrote one day. "Did you ever stop to think how beautiful it can be?"[57] It was not unusual for him to refer to "us Americans"—as in "I guess us Americans must seem a screwball lot" to the Italians.[58] Yet he could not, nor did he wish to, escape his race. Racial awareness and pride, along with cultural distinctiveness, permeate his letters. Coming back from a trip to Pompeii, Italy, while on leave, he noted: "Naturally the passengers were quite curious about us wondering as to our race . . . They couldn't quite figure out how come we were speaking English, when we were Japanese."[59] When visiting Rome a week later he had enjoyed meeting some Japanese students. In Milano a year later he was "intrigued" that the lead soprano in *Madame Butterfly* was Japanese, "a Miss Atsuko." He wrote Hana a long description of his memorable experience at the opera: "Somehow, to see a *'nihonjin'* [Japanese person] receive the plaudits of the audience does my heart good . . . She was extremely graceful in her role and I was proud indeed, and I must have shown it for many of the other listeners seemed to [be] quite amused and curious at our presence."[60] After the performance, they decided to visit the singer backstage, although he reported that he "was *'hazukashii-wa'* [shy]." Learning about Miss Atsuko's life in Rome, he could not help but reflect on the experience of the Nisei in America: "Of course, here there is not that race prejudice encountered back home and, an artist as she, [*sic*] is only judged on her merits and that she has aplenty."[61] His sense of cultural and racial differences was not limited to encounters with civilians. In reference to the

Euro-American men with whom the Nisei soldiers shared some
duties, he casually uses the word "haole"—the Hawaiian term for
a white person or foreigner: "It must be awfully confusing to the
haole litter bearers with us when they hear us talking about *nizakana*
[poached fish] and *buta dofu* [pork tofu], etc. Poor guys, all they
can talk about is steak and chops and roasts. How limited their
capacity as gourmets!"[62]

If Masuda's commentaries about cultural differences were
lighthearted when he described his experience overseas, however,
they were not so when he turned his thoughts to home. Occasionally, a pointed commentary on racial discrimination surfaced in
his correspondence:

> We just read an article in *Stars and Stripes* about Pfc Naito's being
> refused into the Spokane VFW and it's caused a minor furor . . .
> Of late *Yank* and *Stars and Stripes* are going great guns for us,
> and it does us good. If only the people back home could have the
> same viewpoint as the GIs who shared some of our miseries. I
> guess it's up to us to show some of these narrow-minded bigots
> when we get back home.[63]

While criticism of the blatant bigotry of Californians rolled easily
off his tongue, the relative cost and benefit, so to speak, of the
sacrifice made by the Nisei soldiers was a more difficult topic for
him to discuss (and probably to sort out in his own mind). The
Japanese American units received an inordinate number of military honors and publicity, and Masuda often expressed his pride
that their accomplishments were recognized.[64] Yet in his comments on these accolades one discerns a certain critical judgment
that perhaps the cost was too high, and the benefits still uncertain:
"So the 442nd is getting a lot of publicity—we'd been told that
would be so," he wrote on August 17, 1944. "That's good, but at
what cost." He continued with a long description of a recent visit

to a cemetery "where many of our boys lie ... It was with mingled feeling that we went out there and knelt and prayed for these men who had been our brothers, relations and friends ... I didn't mean to be so morbid in this letter—but you just can't ignore the casualties of war."[65] On the eve of Japan's surrender on August 14, 1945, Masuda expressed his hope that "being the unique unit that we are, with all the combat days and publicity behind us, the Army may be prevailed on to give us a break and send us home so that a lot of the boys can go home and help their parents out of relocation centers which close in November."[66] He was to be disappointed. In late November he bitterly wrote from Italy about having been "really snafued up" and left waiting for a ship to take him home.[67]

Masuda's published wartime correspondence is bracketed in a prologue and epilogue by excerpts from a speech and article he published in 1979 on the issue of redress and reparation. He was by then a spokesperson for minority rights and active in several community organizations in Seattle. One of the issues that he took on in these recollections of his war experience was the response to the evacuation. He recalled that vigorous protest by some had been to no avail:

> These were as small voices crying in the wilderness, inundated by the great mass and might of America. If you combine this with the cultural attitudes of fatalism, the acceptance of adversities, and the traditional bowing to authority, we have the answers for the bewildering but adaptive behaviour of the Nikkei [Japanese American] people. They went and they survived.[68]

Masuda was referring here to a set of Japanese cultural values that the scholar Diane C. Fujino has summarized thus: "[There was] no option other than to *gaman* (endure) because there's nothing that can be done, *shikataganai*."[69] In his 1970s recollections, Masuda further described the "submerged anger and bitterness" that his generation felt: refusing to dwell on these feelings was a natural "human defense," for "allowing [them] to surface and bubble would bring forth pain too strong to bear and detract from the goal of survival and achievement in the postwar years."[70] In the epilogue he explained: "I have never repented the decision to volunteer. In retrospect, the war record helped all Nikkei in their postwar struggle." Yet after recalling the "many sad memories of friends who fell in battle," he concluded somewhat ambivalently: "What a price they paid for all of us. And if that is how loyalty is measured, then America got more than its money's worth in their sacrifice."[71]

The "price of loyalty" was high for Japanese Americans and their noncitizen parents. And many chose to renounce their American citizenship in late 1944 and early 1945—in fact, more than four times the number of internees who volunteered for Uncle Sam's army. The motivations of these five thousand or so "renunciants" were as complex as was their legal saga: they may have acted out of pragmatic concerns, rather than loyalty to Japan, and most later asked for repeal of their renunciation. But their little-known story suggests the care with which one must approach the question of national identity. As the historian Mae Ngai, who studied their case, concludes: "The renunciants . . . held complicated, divided loyalties, a set of allegiances that sustained commitment to life in America alongside affective and cultural ties, and even patriotic sympathies, with Japan . . . Their patriotic ties to *both* the U.S. and Japanese nation-states were nevertheless weak."[72]

Masuda's loyalty to the American nation was strong, but so were his affective and cultural ties to the Japanese diaspora. In contrast with the Dietrich correspondence, his contain few dissections of the issues that concern him most. He spoke of racial discrimination in spurts of impatience and anger, but the difficult questions that seemed to cause him the most pain—the cost paid by young men, "our brothers, relations and friends," for a country that bestowed them with military honors yet marginalized and insulted their families—he addressed in muted tones. Although his letters are for the most part non-accusatory, they are evocative of the tremendous sacrifice his country demanded of him.

# 9

## IDENTITIES

In his book *American Crucible*, the historian Gary Gerstle argues that World War II represented a transformative moment for American national identity—a moment when the particular boundaries of civic and racial nationalism shifted. By "civic" nationalism, Gerstle refers to the democratic tradition of equality for all; "racial" nationalism refers to the racially based exclusionary ideologies and practices that coexist with the egalitarian promises of the American republic. During the war, values of "common Americanness" were extended to include previously excluded groups: second-generation immigrants from southern and eastern Europe who in the early part of the century had been considered "racially" distinct from the Protestant majority (partly because they were Catholics and Jews) were now fully integrated into the military and, by extension, into the national community. In contrast, African Americans, like Japanese Americans, saw their exclusion from the mainstream reaffirmed through ongoing discrimination on the home front and segregation in the armed forces.

Gerstle argues that segregation in the armed forces, in particular, had a lasting impact. He uses the examples of Hollywood's combat films and material drawn from veterans' memoirs to illustrate how the boundaries of national citizenship were redrawn by the war. These films typically featured the exploits of the multicultural platoon—"a unit made of Protestants, Catholics, Jews, southerners, westerners, and easterners, all of whom were white"—that achieves its military success through the rallying together of its members in spite of their differences. As he explains, "Thus battle itself . . . is the crucible that transforms [the protagonists] from many individuals into a single fighting force. Their success in these harrowing circumstances depends not simply on their courage as individuals but in their willingness to give themselves entirely to the group, in the process erasing whatever prejudice they may have harboured toward the Jew, the Dago, or the Mick in their bunch." In a context where national unity was reaffirmed through the shared sacrifice born out of combat, the segregation of African and Japanese Americans in the military was of critical importance. As the author further argues in the context of analyzing a Marine veteran's memoir, "The exclusion of blacks from combat platoons . . . denied servicemen . . . the opportunity to challenge and to reconstitute their racially inflected conception of American community. Because of African Americans' absence, [the serviceman] could not learn to include them in his sacred circle as he learned to include Jews, Catholics, and white southerners. In such a way did World War II reinvigorate traditional, racialized notions of America." In sum, the war reshaped national identity to include a broader group of "white" Americans while it entrenched the racial exclusion of African and Japanese Americans.[1]

In the following pages, I examine Gerstle's interpretation in light of recent studies of the war experiences of cultural and racial minorities. How did Jewish Americans negotiate their position in a newly defined "Judeo-Christian" nation? Were Native Americans, who served on an integrated basis in the U.S. military, included in the recently broadened "white" America? How did African Americans' protests against exclusionary practices reflect their demands on the nation and shape their identities? The approaches historians have used in recent years in attempting to answer these questions and the insights their analyses have yielded are the focuses of this essay.

Although anti-Catholic sentiments lingered in 1940s America, Jews were the only group of white Euro-Americans to face open discrimination during World War II. Public opinion surveys expressed overt antisemitic hostility, and quotas on admission to colleges, universities, and professional schools specifically targeted Jewish Americans.[2] In the context of the rise of Nazi antisemitism, a newly formulated Judeo-Christian tradition that aimed at countering these prejudices was popularized in the 1940s, according to the historian Deborah Dash Moore. The vice presidential candidate Henry Wallace was one to formulate this more inclusive view and to present it as *the* American tradition: "The Christians of this land share with the Jews the tradition of the prophets," he wrote in 1940. "This tradition . . . is fundamental to American democracy . . . The Jewish tradition, the Christian tradition, the democratic tradition and the American tradition are all one."[3]

Of course, prejudices against Jews were also found in the armed forces, an institution that was gentile in practice, as illustrated by the inclusion of pork (a forbidden food according to Jewish dietary laws) in standard GI meals. Formally, however, the military leadership embraced the inclusiveness of the Judeo-Christian principle by promoting ecumenical relations among Jews and Christians. Specifically, the armed forces issued directives to include Judaism along with Protestantism and Catholicism in the religious services offered under its standard operating procedure. Even chaplains' schools implemented integration programs by assigning students of different faiths to the same dormitory suites. Moore studied how individual servicemen navigated these mixed waters. (More than half a million Jewish Americans served in the armed forces.) Her conclusions—that their war experience accentuated their awareness of both their Americanness and their Jewishness—supports Gerstle's analysis of a broadened definition of national identity, but it also provides evidence of an enduring sense of distinctiveness on the part of an important segment of the new "white" America.

Jews who fought in the American army felt "equal to other Americans" and identified "the democratic ideals of the United States with their own Jewish values," explained the author in an article published in 1998, at an early stage in her research. She then put the emphasis on the egalitarian and inclusive Judeo-Christian creed—"Jews and Christians were equally Americans; both were members of a Judeo-Christian nation"—and suggested that it reflected the experience of many Jewish American GIs. As stated with evident satisfaction by a navy chaplain: "My Judaism and my Americanism are here so organically interwoven and so complement each other that I enjoy peace of mind and peace of soul."[4] In her book *GI Jews*, published in 2004, Moore further documents this integrationist moment by following the journey of fifteen servicemen. Her collective biography reasserts the main theme of her previous work—that Jews were integrated into the American nation during the war—but it also emphasizes the recognition of Jewish differences. Jewish servicemen were reminded of their distinctiveness when confronted with antisemitic prejudices, including stereotypes of physical weakness, cowardice, and avarice.[5] More positively, they were aware that their "profound revulsion against fascism" distinguished them from other soldiers who did not fight out of ideological motivation. "Most Americans in December 1941 considered Japan the archenemy, unlike American Jews, who targeted Hitler as the important foe," explains the author. It was "their war."[6] Thus, while the experience of worshipping and fighting together forged a common bond,[7] it did not erase their sense of distinctiveness as Jews. The path taken after the war by the men Moore followed in her collective biography—some supported Palestinian Jews in their struggle for a Jewish state, others fought to eradicate antisemitic restrictions at home and to assist African Americans in their struggle for civil rights—also illustrated an enduring Jewish consciousness. "Military service had empowered Jews as Americans and as Jews," concluded Moore.[8]

The experience of Native Americans offers a second case in which the integrationist meaning of the war can be examined. American Indians occupy a unique status in, and in relation to, the United States.[9] Economically, they constituted a particularly disadvantaged group. In 1939, the median income for all Indian males living on reservations was $500, compared to a median income of $2,300 for all males living in the United States. At a time when the national unemployment rate was 15 percent, one-third of all Indian males living off reservations were unemployed. The average life expectancy for Indians in 1940 was thirty to thirty-four years, compared with sixty to sixty-four years for the country at large. Their access to formal education was also substandard: nearly one-quarter of all Indian males had no schooling, compared to 8 percent of the black population and just 1 percent of the total male population.[10]

In addition to their marginal economic status, Native Americans' relation to the American nation was complicated by political discrimination and ambiguity resulting from their dual citizenship. In 1924, Congress granted citizenship to all Native Americans who were not yet enfranchised, but seven states still refused to let Indians vote in 1938. It was only in the summer of 1948 that Arizona and New Mexico, with respectively the second- and third-largest Indian populations in the United States, were forced by court order to lift the restrictions on voting rights imposed on their Indian citizens.[11] American citizenship, such as it was, coexisted with the recognition of tribal sovereignty. The negotiation of treaties between the United States and various groups of Native peoples assumed political sovereignty. By 1939 the United States had systematically violated its treaties with the Native tribes and, within the course of a half century, unilaterally imposed successive policies to break up (the Dawes Act of 1887), then reconstitute (the Indian Reorganization Act of 1934), tribal relationships. Native Americans, often divided among themselves on the relative benefit or danger of assimilation, thus stood in a peculiar relationship to the American nation.[12]

In spite of that torturous relationship, Native Americans responded to the war much like their non-Indian counterparts—for the most part, enthusiastically. Support for the war effort on the home front was extensive. Not only did individuals and tribes purchase war bonds, but many tribal councils made their resources available to the American government for the duration of the war. Native Americans also worked in the war industry: approximately forty thousand, one-fifth of all able-bodied Indian women, left reservations for war-related work.[13] Some resistance to the draft took place, but close to half of the reservation Indians served in the military. Had Indian health and literacy levels been greater, noted Kenneth Townsend, the participation of Native Americans would have been higher, since one-third of all Indians who sought enlistment were rejected.[14] On the whole, it was thus as patriotic Americans that Native Americans responded to the war emergency. It was also, according to official military policy, as "whites" that they served, in contrast with African and Japanese Americans, who were confined to segregated units. Commissioner of Indian Affairs John Collier had lobbied for an all-Indian division administered by the Bureau of Indian Affairs, but military leaders rejected his proposal. "[The] War Department feels that the proper policy governing the assignment and training of the Indian under the Selective Service should be the same as for the white trainee," replied Secretary of War Henry Stimson.[15]

While Native Americans proved themselves willing to serve the American cause with which they identified, they also used the opportunity created by the war to reassert their long-standing quest for national self-determination. The Iroquois Confederacy (or Six Nations) did so most forcefully when it legally challenged the application of the draft to its members in 1940. The Confederacy argued that as a distinct nation they were not subject to American laws, including the draft and previous statutes such as the 1924 Citizenship Act. They lost their court case on appeal in November 1941. Six months later, in June 1942, they resorted to a symbolic gesture by issuing their own declaration of war against the enemies of the United States. The ceremony was held on the steps of the Capitol Building in the presence of Vice President Henry Wallace and broadcast on national radio. By declaring themselves allies of the United States, the Iroquois leaders were reaffirming their claim to sovereignty and their willingness to fight alongside the white nation.[16] Native Americans again attempted to remind their white neighbors of their special status in 1944 when leaders from across the United States met to form what became a lasting political coalition, the first of its kind: the National Congress of American Indians (NCAI). In a context where the contributions and exploits of Indian fighters in Uncle Sam's army were receiving extensive publicity and were used as proof of their readiness, and willingness, to be assimilated into white society, Native leaders felt the need to organize to counter the assimilationist trends unleashed by the war.[17] As summarized by Alison Bernstein in her 1991 examination of the question, their position was that "individuals could be both American Indians and Indian Americans, and . . . they should not be forced to give up their cultural identity [and tribal autonomy] to enjoy the rights and responsibilities of citizenship." After the war, in spite of the Native Americans' efforts to regain control over their individual and collective destiny while asserting their belonging to the American nation,

Congress proceeded with the "termination" of the tribes' special status and of all federal responsibilities for the tribes, including those agreed upon through treaties. Enacted in 1954, the policy was the direct brainchild of wartime assimilationist pressures.[18]

Scholars' assessments of the "integrated" experience of Native Americans during the war is, on the whole, positive. Bernstein presents their service in the military as "an unparalleled opportunity to compete in the white world in an arena where their talents and reputation as fighters inspired respect." Likewise, the common practice to nickname Native servicemen "Chief" was not particularly suggestive of white prejudice, in her estimation: it "signified something other than condescension; it signified respect." It was received, she argued, as a sign of friendship and acceptance. Although she recognized that "whites occasionally got carried away with the Indian warrior image," her narrative emphasized the equality shared by Indian and non-Indian servicemen.[19] Writing a decade later, Kenneth Townsend agreed: "The positive attention and the warm reception given Indians by white soldiers and their officers indicated a ready acceptance of Native Americans in the armed forces." Especially in comparison to the extensive and systematic discrimination faced by African Americans, the "curiosity" expressed toward Native Americans was benign. Discussing Native participation in the urban workforce, Townsend further argued that the intensity of antiblack racism "gave evidence to Native Americans of their own acceptance among whites. The sweeping positive reception accorded to Indians in the nation's labor force and in community social settings all pointed to that assessment." As in Bernstein's, in Townsend's narrative the war constitutes a high point in the Native Americans' relationship to the white nation: "Never before did full inclusion with white society seem so possible . . . The war generated an atmosphere of optimism among American Indians, a feeling of equality and a perception of opportunity . . . They held the faith that once peace returned, Indians would be in a position to determine for themselves the postwar direction of their own lives."[20]

Jere' Bishop Franco is less sanguine in her assessment of whites' respect and acceptance of Native American servicemen. Citing a veteran who served under a Native American sergeant, she notes his recollection that "we never called him ['Chief'] because we wanted to respect him." In regard to Native integration into the off-reservation workforce, she describes how traditional tribal customs conflicted with white values and how cultural misunderstandings and prejudices created an environment inhospitable to Native workers. On the whole, however, Franco's account of the wartime experience of western tribes follows a fairly familiar interpretive path largely framed by the integrationist paradigm.[21]

A more strongly dissonant note on the meaning of the war for Native communities is heard through Carol Miller's reading of Native fiction. As she summarizes her disagreement with the main interpretation reviewed above: "From the official federal perspective, and certainly for some Indian groups and individuals as well, the war provided an extraordinary stimulus toward assimilation, a goal some welcomed as inevitable and desirable. But for many others the war also engendered a cultural subversion resulting not in emancipation and inclusion but in exile and disillusion." Dislocation is the theme that dominates her account. "In addition to the immediate cost in injury and loss of life," Miller further explains, "the war precipitated other damaging consequences to the cultural stability of Native people. Military service and relocation to urban areas were supposed to hasten assimilation by weakening tribal ties, and that is precisely what happened."[22] Her perspective is supported by the well-documented losses experienced by Native Americans in the postwar period that all authors, including those who stress the hopes and possibilities of the war period, cite. Although the average income of Native Americans increased by two and one-half times between 1940 and 1944, not only did it remain significantly lower than that of non-Indians during the war, but it plummeted after 1946.[23] When Native servicemen and urban workers returned to their reservations in 1945 and 1946, they found reduced acreage, deteriorated services, and stagnant economies. The federal government purchased Indian land for airbases, aerial gunnery ranges, and other wartime uses; the terms were sometimes advantageous to the tribes, sometimes not. Overall, almost a million fewer acres were under tribal ownership by 1945. Treaty allotments had been suspended during the war, and as a result, services had deteriorated and reservation economies were in shambles. As reported by Bernstein, and in accord with Miller's interpretation, the postwar pattern that quickly emerged revealed the communal uprooting of Native Americans: "Even though most Indians initially returned [to the reservation], many became quickly discouraged and left, only to reappear months later after unsuccessful attempts to readjust to life in the non-Indian world." The status of off-reservation Natives further illustrates the substandard status that Native Americans were unable to shake off in spite of their wartime contribution. "Sadly," concluded Bernstein, "urban Indians gained few lasting economic advantages. The median income in 1949 for urban male Indians was $1,198 as contrasted with $950 for reservation-based Indians, $2,218 for black males, and $3,780 for whites. Indians had even less education and higher unemployment than blacks, a phenomenon that persists to this day."[24] Native Americans might have served as "whites" during the war, but their "assimilation" suggested dynamics of racial marginalization and exploitation, not integration as full and respected members of the American nation.

As the nation's largest racial minority, African Americans played a special role in the war, and that experience profoundly shaped their ongoing struggle for civil rights and economic justice. More than one million African Americans served in the United States armed forces, but in spite of vocal and sustained criticism by black leaders, the contribution of black soldiers, unlike that of Jewish and Native American servicemen, was channeled through segregated units and predominantly noncombat activities. As described by Christopher Paul Moore, most black servicemen were assigned to service, construction, and transportation units. "Black soldiers were not generally asked to carry guns, but they were ordered to carry nearly everything else . . . They built bases, airfields, and roads. They transported artillery, ammunition, troops, and airplanes. They drained swamps and shorelines for docks and piers." They were also assigned to the particularly gruesome work of graves registration service. Only late in the war did some instances of integration take place in the service.[25] On the home front, in spite of some federal efforts to prohibit discrimination in the war industry and in spite of the urgent need for manpower after 1943, economic discrimination persisted.[26] Political disenfranchisement continued to be the norm in the South, and eruptions of racial violence shook northern cities.[27] A nascent civil rights movement protested America's democratic flaws, but no victory was in sight. As recently summarized by the historian Thomas Sugrue, the demands presented by wartime civil rights leaders were far-reaching: "They embraced a vision of democracy that was far broader than the narrow notion of individual civil rights: They demanded the full economic and political rights of citizenship. This meant inclusion in American institutions that had long excluded blacks or relegated them to second-class status, as well as the embrace of a rhetoric of rights that encompassed the right to a decent job, to a decent home, and to economic security. They were the vanguard of an unachieved American democracy." Full inclusion in the nation's economic and political institutions—not just access to formal civil rights—was the goal to which they aspired, and it eluded them.[28]

As Sugrue points out, many black leaders who demanded fair treatment and inclusion did so from a position of deep skepticism about the rhetoric of freedom that dominated their government's official propaganda.[29] The promises of American democracy not only sounded hollow but were hollow for African Americans, who knew that the "myth" of the American Creed was often just that. Maureen Honey's compilation of black women's prose and poetry, *Bitter Fruit*, richly illustrates this sentiment. In African American wartime fiction, explained Honey, irony is omnipresent. Several compelling examples can be cited, for instance, Gwendolyn Williams's short story "Heart Against the Wind." In fictional letters to her husband, Stephen, who is in the service, Lys announces that they are expecting a baby. The first letter includes an acerbic confession that she does not want to give birth to a child who "has no country," a "step-citizen" for whom "Gettysburg, July the Fourth, and constitutional rights are ashes." That letter is trashed, to be replaced by a shorter one, more in line with the forced optimism of the time: "We are going to be the proud parents . . . of a very special citizen. Don't worry about me, everything is going swell." Zora L. Barnes in "Portrait of a Citizen" uses a similar device. A young man about to report for service writes to his sweatheart: "Four days from now I'll have on a uniform and *I'll be a citizen!* . . . I'm not a praying man and now I'll have even less time to learn how, but my darling while you're praying for our little dreams to come true will you say something about hoping that after I get out of that uniform . . . the 'citizen' part will stick?"[30]

Some authors have turned to marginal expressions of protest— some from within the service, some from without—to illustrate the complexity of the African American response to the war. In their history *The First Strange Place*, Beth Bailey and David Farber chose the unique context of Hawaii to capture moments when black servicemen engaged in direct acts of resistance. Soldiers of the 369th Coast Regiment (an antiaircraft artillery unit) were an elite and proud group known as the "Harlem Hellfighters" who did not take racial humiliation passively. They fought back when confronted by white sailors and soldiers who insulted them on the streets of Honololu and made sure that their black officers received proper salutes from white subordinates. Their experience was not typical, but it illustrated the possibility offered by military service, at least in some exceptional circumstances, to imagine alternative social arrangements.[31]

Resisters of a different kind were the "zoot suiters," who, as Robin Kelley has described in the case of the young Malcolm Little (later X), represented a culture of opposition among young African and Mexican Americans. Whether they lived in Harlem or in Los Angeles, like those who were attacked and "de-zooted" (literally stripped of their clothes) by white sailors in early June 1943, these "hep cats" who donned oversized jackets and draped pants tapered at the ankle, along with polished shoes and the signature broad-brimmed hat, violated every aspect of America's sacrificial ethos: they flouted fabric restrictions, eluded the draft, and refused to set foot in a munitions factory. According to the historian Luis Alvarez, zoot suit culture offered its participants self-validation; it "opened spaces of autonomy and independence for many of the youth involved."[32] In a language informed by cultural criticism, Alvarez wrote that "zoot suiters *mobilized* their bodies" to "challenge the indignities forced upon them." They rejected the assimilationist paradigm in a flamboyant and unmistakable way.

Racial and cultural minorities negotiated their place in the white nation in multiple and complex ways during World War II. As Gary Gerstle has noted in *American Crucible*, the war propelled a redefinition of national identity that included previously excluded "white ethnics." Racialized groups, regardless of their relative contribution to the war effort as civilians or in the service, found their exclusion from the national community reaffirmed. The wartime democratic rhetoric and aspirations might have inspired movements of protest among excluded groups, such as the modern African American civil rights movement and the National Congress of American Indians, but these groups faced decades of struggle before meaningful equality and respect would be achieved. Military service, Gerstle suggested, and particularly the bare necessity of survival in combat situations, created affective bonds that made it possible to imagine a more inclusive national community. But as the postwar marginalization of Native Americans suggests, more than wartime respect for "Chiefs" would be needed to enlarge the national "sacred circle."

# COMMENTARY
### by Robert D. Johnston

The short introduction to part III inspired me to think about this book as a whole. For now we can clearly see that Sylvie Murray made a fairly astounding choice—really a set of choices—about what subject matter she'd be covering. We learn here of isolationism, patriotic propaganda, and the gender of patriotic sacrifice, along with stories of Jews, blacks, and persons of Japanese ancestry.

But we do not get *battles*, nor do we read diplomats' cables. We aren't going to learn about the way in which the Battle of Midway proved to be a turning point of the war. We won't hear anything about the problem of a second front in the European theater. The dropping of the atomic bomb will receive no attention, nor will crucial diplomatic moments such as the conference at Yalta.

Can a scholar really write a history of World War II without exploring these critically important events and issues? Most assuredly so. I am firmly on Murray's side in finding the greatest overall significance in the study of American involvement in World War II in the areas of social, cultural, and political history. I mean to take nothing away from the bravery of the soldiers involved, or from the thoughtfulness and creativity of the military historians who have reconstructed the war's big battles. Yet the livelier, more complex, and more difficult interpretive issues that historians face do seem to relate to the more domestic-oriented histories that Murray presents.

That said, Murray's fundamental choice—to radically subordinate military and diplomatic history—is a choice that not all scholars would be comfortable with. Moreover, I do wish that Murray had spoken at greater length about *why* she chose to focus on various subjects, and why she believed that those subjects would produce a volume more valuable than a different World War II book about different subjects. Perhaps she could have discussed the topics that nearly made it into the book but ultimately got left on the cutting room floor. Or she might have explored how she decided to ignore topics (such as the atomic bomb) that are, after all, of perennial interest to historians and students alike.

Even without such explicit commentary from Murray, however, you can take her up on her invitation to determine whether you approve of her selection of subjects. Would you have made the same choices? Might you instead have written a more traditional history? Or might you have even taken a book about World War II in more nontraditional, subversive directions?

We do need to recognize, however, that even though battles do not figure in Murray's work, the book does include the experience of *combat*. Or, to be more precise, *writing about combat*. For chapter 7 is a meditation on, first, the writings of the war correspondent Ernie Pyle, and second, the impossibility of truly conveying the horrors of warfare to noncombatants. I appreciate what Murray is trying to do here, and she appropriately celebrates the grim and determined Pyle as a "Walt Whitman of the twentieth century." Yet the larger argument remains, to my mind, elusive. Murray doesn't really try to prove her thesis, but rather offers suggestive insights into why writers were not able to portray to the audience back home the intense reality of combat. I would, however, have liked to see a more systematic defense of this interpretation.

Also, I would have preferred some exploration of related issues that transcend the specific issue of representing wartime combat. Can, for example, a historian truly convey the inner reality of the worldview of thirteenth-century heretics? Can an anthropologist truly convey the inner reality of cultural practices quite different from our own? Can a novelist truly convey the inner relationship between lover and beloved? The issues that Murray raises are, in the end, deeply human questions about communication and the ability to "know" others, and so a more extended meditation would have been a valuable addendum to her treatment. (To be sure, and in Murray's defense, almost all scholarly historians—unfortunately, I think—shy away from such philosophical musings.)

We do get deeply human material in the eighth chapter. I was quite moved by the experiences, and the letter writing, of the main protagonists—Minoru Masuda and the Dietrich brothers, Frank and Albert. In a brief space, Murray evocatively portrays these characters. We especially get a vivid sense of the lifeline that correspondence provided to them. The

Dietrich brothers engaged in an amazing epistolary discussion of loyalty, patriotism, war, and peace—showing, among other things, the intellectual and political vitality of ordinary people.

Masuda is no less amazing, as is the story of his fellow soldiers who, having had their constitutional rights trampled upon, might understandably have said "Take this country and shove it." The most poignant moment in his letters comes when Masuda is desperately trying to get home from Europe after his valorous combat—so that he can help his parents move out of the relocation camps. Just imagine the intense, but surely ambivalent, loyalty that Masuda must have felt for this country at such a moment, and how difficult it must have been when he learned that a snafu would prevent him from making it home in time. Perhaps this can help us better understand why some Americans of Japanese ancestry did tell the country to "shove it." As Murray notes, approximately five thousand renounced their citizenship—four times as many as volunteered for military service. This is a delicate subject that most Americans still dance around in "muted tones." Fortunately, scholars are increasingly pointing to the complexities of the political responses of camp internees, which varied across generation and across time.[1] I don't think it would have undermined her concentration on Masuda for Murray to have spent just a bit more time exploring these matters.

Murray extends her treatment of excluded groups in the final substantive chapter as she takes on the question of wartime identity for Jews, Native Americans, and African Americans. Playing off Gary Gerstle's important *American Crucible*, Murray does a fine job of revealing the complex identities that all three groups constructed in the face of both wartime discrimination and opportunity. I do wish, though, that Murray had here presented stronger theses. Perhaps she did not do so because she wants to respect the complexity of the history involved, the historians who have written about these groups, and you, her readers, who can make up your minds for yourselves. But I would still like to have seen a forceful statement from Murray for each group.

Finally, I would also have preferred to have a clearer answer to the question that is implicit here and that Murray in her conclusion acknowledges is left unanswered even though it "is particularly dear to historians"—namely: Did the war propel a substantial change in social relations, or did it strengthen elements of continuity already at work in American society? This is quite an important matter, as both citizens and scholars alike seek to learn the origins of contemporary racial equality (and inequality). To put it baldly: Do we have a gruesome, violent, total war to thank for the modern civil rights movement?

## CONCLUSION

Through a selection of essay topics and formats, this book has told parts of a much broader story. In conclusion, we briefly review the main contour of the historical narrative presented here, and some of its omissions, and we highlight the interpretive choices that have shaped it. Since the goal of this book was to invite students to think critically about historical writing, including their own writing, it is fitting to close the book on a self-assessment by the author.

Part I examines America's response to the advance of Nazi Germany in Europe. Even after the fall of Belgium, Luxembourg, the Netherlands, and France in the spring and summer of 1940, public and congressional opinion resisted taking active steps to support the largest remaining European democracy, Britain, also under direct fire by early September. The adoption of the Lend-Lease Act in March 1941 marked a turning point in the United States' support for the Allies, but, as we examined in chapter 2, it was preceded by a sharp debate, and the opposition to aid short of war persisted among a cross section of the American public until the attack on Pearl Harbor.

The debate over intervention is revealing of the strong nationalist current that ran through American political culture: the question most prominent in these days was not whether the United States should rush to the protection of civilians in the countries under Nazi occupation, but whether national security—and by implication the national interest—was endangered by the military conflict raging in Europe. While interventionists argued that it was, and thus that aid to Britain was essential to stopping Hitler's advance, anti-interventionists refused to concede the point. As we saw in chapter 1, a realist tone characterized presidential rhetoric in particular. Although Roosevelt expressed the humanitarian goal of defending the "four essential human freedoms . . . everywhere in the world" in his January 1941 address to Congress, such a call was not typical of his pre–Pearl Harbor public addresses, nor did it inspire the citizenry to take up arms until American territories came under direct attack. It was Norman Rockwell in 1943, not Franklin Roosevelt in 1941, who implanted the idealism of the "Four Freedoms" in the American public imagination.

In part I the focus rested on the response to the European war. This does not mean, of course, that the broadening conflict in Asia was of no concern to Americans, especially after Japan occupied Nanking, China's capital city, in late 1937, and began waging full-scale war in the region. When in September 1940 Japan signed a military alliance with Germany and Italy, the global nature of the crisis was unmistakable. But the administration trod carefully—the nation was not willing or ready to wage war, let alone on two fronts.[1]

My decision to focus on Europe and ignore Asia, as with most interpretive choices, was made largely out of necessity—space restriction did not allow for an exhaustive treatment of all aspects of America's responses to mounting aggression in the world. There is also a certain historical logic to the choice made. One could argue, for instance, that Europe remained the main focus of attention and debate between 1939 and December 1941. Manfred Jonas advanced this position when he noted that anti-interventionists were less concerned about multilateral commitments in Asia than they were about Europe. In a war against Japan, he explained, "the United States could function quite independently and ran no risk of having its wartime or postwar politics 'dictated' by powerful allies. In Europe, on the other hand, war would mean a *de facto* alliance with Great Britain and France, and thus raise the spectre of substantial and perhaps permanent entanglement in European affairs." Similarly, the historian Richard W. Steele argued that President Roosevelt was for the most part silent on events in Asia throughout 1940 and 1941: "The result was that insofar as Americans depended on the president and the mass media for their political education, they were ignorant of the circumstances that would explain the attack on Pearl Harbor and that would catapult the nation into World War II."[2] The choice to give privileged attention to the presidential public addresses in chapter 1 and to anti-interventionism in chapter 2 thus reinforces the Eurocentric bias of our narrative. Yet including America's relationship to Asia in our assessment of the pre–Pearl Harbor period could have opened productive lines of inquiry. Was the advance of antidemocratic regimes assessed differently in the cases of Europe and Asia? America's racialized views of East Asians were as deep as its antisemitism. How did they color the response to Japanese aggression?[3]

Finally, consideration of the place that the attack on Pearl Harbor occupies in public remembrances and professional interpretations of the war would have added to chapter 3's analysis of the war's "obligatory goodness." The cultural historian Emily Rosenberg has examined the variety of "memories/histories" that have been constructed out of the essentially defensive and vengeful impulse inspired by the December 7 attack.[4] But how do the multifaceted, sometimes contradictory narratives that she dissects converge with, or diverge from, the humanitarian narrative of the European war, or Nicholson Baker's attempt to subvert this paradigm?

Where in this ongoing process of remembering and interpreting the American experience of World War II should we situate recent "history/memory" productions such as Ken Burns's *The War* (2007) or HBO's *The Pacific* (2010)?

The attack on Pearl Harbor profoundly changed the tenor of public discussion in America. The country's responsibility to defend the free world and its citizens' duty to support the war effort were now proclaimed on every imaginable public space, from theater screens to billboards. Chapter 4 examines some of the material that shaped this public culture, chapter 5 questions the argument that wartime rhetoric is illustrative of the "privatized" essence of American political culture, and chapter 6 explores how the language of "sacrifice" applied differently to women, who were expected to "serve" but not to "fight for" their country. In all of these essays, the emphasis is on the producers of culture: the writers, illustrators, filmmakers, commercial artists, and other opinion makers who, along with their superiors in the Office of War Information, the armed forces, and private corporations, gave meaning to the war effort. The visual and rhetorical environment they created, these essays assume, reflected national values—or, to paraphrase Robert Westbrook, Americans' felt obligation to their country. Whether the values revealed by this "popular patriotism" were genuinely political and national, or rather private or even transnational, is a debate we need not reopen here. However, it is worth considering other shapers of political culture left out of the narrative presented in part II.

Students of political culture are interested in the attitudes, beliefs, and values that underpin the workings of a particular political community, often a nation-state. These ideas also set the parameters of membership in, or allegiance to, a political community. How was inclusion in, and exclusion from, the American political community conceived during World War II? The answer provided by official propaganda and disseminated through the mass media was, simplified to its lowest common denominator, willingness to sacrifice for the war effort. This criterion was qualified in dozens of ways in the material produced to "create a will to win," but in essence the message was that one's status, rights, and privileges as a citizen were contingent on one's commitment to the national emergency at hand.[5]

Mass media occupy such a salient place in twentieth-century culture that it is easy to leave it at that—to let publicity steal the show, so to speak. But the words and actions of policy makers and administrators are also revealing of the cultural makeup of a society. Scholarship on modern American citizenship, especially in the area of welfare policies, has highlighted the connections that existed between culture and policy—between the ideas about gender roles and racial identity held by legislators, for instance, and the provision of governmental assistance through social security measures. Assumptions about family obligations and racial inferiority have directly informed the shaping of the Social Security Act, they argue, and in turn, that important legislative intervention has reinforced societal values.[6] The methodology employed by these scholars—the rich blend of policy, social, and cultural analysis they deploy—should inspire examinations of wartime political culture. How did the formulation and implementation of the Selective Training and Service Act, for instance, reflect values central to American political culture? How did it shape citizens' felt obligation to the state? A vast scholarship exists on the policies and administrative practices put in place to mobilize resources for war, be they military or civilian, productive or consumptive. How this maze of regulatory action reflected and affected the political culture of the nation at war could lend itself to revealing historical investigation.[7]

Political culture has also been examined in part II apart from the socioeconomic context in which ordinary citizens experienced the war. The economic opportunities that the war industry offered, or denied; the social tensions generated by the geographic mobility, and attending dislocation, of large number of civilians; the personal and collective assertions of worth, or the sufferance of indignities, that accompanied citizens' contributions to the patriotic effort—these are only some elements of the broader historical context left largely unexamined in this volume. An exhaustive scholarship exists on the domestic home front, and to offer a comprehensive coverage of that history was not our purpose; still, the specific historical circumstances through which the war was experienced also gave meaning to the texts produced by propagandists. Thus, any "reading" of posters or advertisements is always partial unless subject to a critical analysis of its reception by individuals or groups of citizens who experienced the war in ways that were not only complex and diverse but also often ambivalent.

It is this multifaceted and varied experience of war—or, more accurately, the multiple experiences of war—that part III seeks to capture. In contrast to a popular and scholarly narrative that stresses the unity of purpose and the forces of homogenization at work in American society, the last three essays examine dissonant voices. The uncertainty that many felt in their relation to the nation is captured through the words of those who spoke from the margins, or of others who spoke on their behalf. Ironically, as we suggest in chapter 7, the military personnel who encountered the war at its most intense—on the front line—struggled to define their place in a nation that glorified their sacrifice, or so was the perspective of popular columnist Ernie Pyle. Other groups were faced with contradictory denial and assertion of their loyalty. Assumed to be treacherous, Japanese Americans were conscripted; that many among them volunteered to fight for Uncle Sam in spite of this affront to their integrity is illustrative of the complex nature of patriotic loyalty. Not dissimilarly, the minority of Americans who rejected compulsory military service out of a conscientious objection to war—some also rejected civilian service for the same reason—encountered social ostracism even though legal provisions had been made for their dissent. Chapter 8 turns to the private letters of individuals caught in this maze to shed light on the gray areas of wartime experience. Finally, chapter 9 moves from the individual to the collective level to examine how the integration of Jewish, Native, and African Americans into the national community was uneven at best. While the first two groups fought alongside gentile Euro-American servicemen, for instance, the latter's segregated and subordinated status was reaffirmed.

One question left unexamined in part III is particularly dear to historians: Did the war propel a substantial change in social relations, or did it strengthen elements of continuity already at work in American society? The debate about whether the war represented a "watershed" or, conversely, whether the changes introduced were "for the duration only" has raged for some time now. Did the war reinforce or disrupt existing relations among Americans of different gender, culture, or race? Did it transform America's political culture or Americans' sense of themselves as members of a national community? Understanding an event's long-term impact and assessing a particular moment's location in the trajectory of historical change is a delicate enterprise—one that entails general familiarity with, and sometimes close analysis of, the periods before and after the moment examined. Thus, answering the questions raised above would require reviewing the recent literature on racial and gender relations in the postwar period and positioning the trends detected in wartime in that broader context. Similarly, returning to the topic that part I of this volume left unresolved, one could ask: Did the war lead to a significant reorientation of America's sense of itself in the world? If so, when did the transition from a nationalist to an internationalist stance take place, and what particular type of commitment was deemed desirable? The answer to the first question is usually affirmative, but immersing ourselves in the moment when sharp disagreements were voiced about the latter would no doubt have a great deal to teach us.

This book is meant to illustrate, through a set of essays accompanied by critical commentaries and self-criticism, the processes involved in the writing of history. Rather than doing so in a decontextualized fashion, or in a multitude of contexts, we have chosen to situate ourselves in a particular moment and place: World War II in America. If this book has been successful, it has demonstrated the critical role that interpretive choices play in the writing of history and will have advanced our historical understanding of this most important period in our recent past by providing suggestive insights into the topics selected.

# AFTERWORD
## by Robert D. Johnston

Murray's conclusion reminds us of the work's, and the author's, major strengths: intelligence, humility, thoughtfulness, and dedication to pluralism. Murray asks us to think about the many omissions in her book, and about the many choices that made this, for example, a book that focused on Europe rather than Asia or that did not look intensively at changes in the U.S. economy. She is honest in acknowledging the many different ways that scholars—and students—can, and do, construct histories of World War II.

And that honest, pluralist message should be an important and empowering one today. We unfortunately live in a divisive, no-holds-barred political culture in which recognition of complexity is taken for weakness and far too many people believe that on any particular issue there is only One True Story. In the end, then, we must be grateful to Sylvie Murray for her gentle subversion of these perilous tendencies, as well as for the model she provides to all of us for a more democratic way of thinking, and being, in the world.

# NOTES

## COMMENTATOR'S NOTE

1. James W. Loewen, *Lies My Teacher Told Me*, second ed. (New York: Touchstone, 2007 [1995]), 8.

## PART I: BEFORE PEARL HARBOR

1. For an introduction to the genre of textbook analysis, see Sara Evans and Roy Rosenzweig, "Textbooks and Teaching: Introduction," *Journal of American History* 78, no. 4 (March 1992).

## 1: IN THE NAME OF NATIONAL SECURITY

1. Lawrence W. and Cornelia Levine, *The People and the President: America's Conversation with FDR* (Boston: Beacon Press, 2002), 341–42. Michael S. Sherry, *In the Shadow of War: The United States Since the 1930s* (New Haven, Conn.: Yale University Press, 1995), 33.
2. An excellent analysis of Roosevelt's foreign policy that takes into account the domestic constraints is Robert Dallek, *Franklin D. Roosevelt and American Foreign Policy, 1932–1945* (New York: Oxford University Press, 1995 [1979]).
3. His public speeches and addresses can be found at www.presidency.ucsb.edu.

4. Kenneth S. Davis, *FDR: Into the Storm, 1937–1940* (New York: Random House, 1993), 550. Levine, *The People and the President*, 287–88.

5. Samuel I. Rosenman, ed., *The Public Papers and Addresses of Franklin D. Roosevelt*, 1940 volume (New York: Macmillan, 1941), xxx.

6. David S. Wyman, *Paper Walls: America and the Refugee Crisis, 1938–1941* (Amherst: University of Massachusetts Press, 1968), 168–69. A total of 250,000 refugees from Nazism reached safety in the United States from 1933 to 1945. The American population was then 130 million.

7. Ibid., 97.

8. Deborah E. Lipstadt, *Beyond Belief: The American Press and the Coming of the Holocaust, 1933–1945* (New York: Free Press, 1986); Laurel Leff, *Buried by "The Times": The Holocaust and America's Most Important Newspaper* (New York: Cambridge University Press, 2005).

9. Dallek, *Franklin D. Roosevelt and American Foreign Policy*, 168, 336. The classic works on this issue, besides *Paper Walls*, cited above, are Henry L. Feingold, *The Politics of Rescue: The Roosevelt Administration and the Holocaust, 1938–1945* (New Brunswick, N.J.: Rutgers University Press, 1970), and David S. Wyman, *The Abandonment of the Jews: America and the Holocaust, 1941–1945* (New York: Pantheon, 1984).

10. Quoted in Feingold, *The Politics of Rescue*, 135.

11. Ibid., 82.

12. Lipstadt, *Beyond Belief*, 128.

13. Feingold, *The Politics of Rescue*, 160.

## 2: THE GREAT DEBATE

1. Justus D. Doenecke, "U.S. Policy and the European War, 1939–1941," *Diplomatic History* 19, no. 4 (1995): 670–71.

2. Justus D. Doenecke, *Storm on the Horizon: The Challenge to American Intervention, 1939–1941* (Lanham, Md.: Rowman and Littlefield, 2003 [2000]), 8. For a shorter book that also shows the diversity of anti-interventionist arguments and includes a selection of documents, see Justus D. Doenecke, *The Battle Against Intervention, 1939–1941* (Malabar, Fla.: Krieger Publishing Company, 1997).

3. Doenecke, *Storm on the Horizon*, 323. Mark A. Stoler, "Avoiding Entry into World War II," *Diplomatic History* 27, no. 2 (April 2003): 283. The persistence of these stereotypes has also been noted by John E. Moser in a review

of *Storm on the Horizon* published in *H-Diplo, H-Net* (April 2001), www
.h-net.org/reviews/showrev.php?id=5082. For a review of Doenecke's book
that notes its challenge to the view of the Good War, although not entirely
approvingly, see Thomas Alan Schwartz, "FDR: Architect of the American
Empire?" *Reviews in American History* 31 (2003): 152–60. The Nazis' propaganda arm did extend to the United States, as it did in other countries,
through the German embassies and the German American Bund, but the
threat of internal subversion, while genuinely feared by Roosevelt and used
to discredit the opponents of intervention, was exaggerated. By 1939, the
Bund had collapsed, though it lingered with two thousand members until
December 1941. See Sander A. Diamond, *The Nazi Movement in the United
States, 1924–1941* (Ithaca, N.Y.: Cornell University Press, 1974), and Alton
Frye, *Nazi Germany and the American Hemisphere, 1933–1941* (New Ha-
ven, Conn.: Yale University Press, 1967). Several scholars in addition to
Doenecke have demonstrated that anti-interventionism was a mainstream
phenomenon shared by a cross section of loyal Americans, not by a few dupes
or traitors. See Wayne S. Cole, *Roosevelt and the Isolationists: 1932–1945*
(Lincoln: University of Nebraska Press, 1983); Manfred Jonas, *Isolationism
in America, 1935–1941* (Ithaca, N.Y.: Cornell University Press, 1966); and
James C. Schneider, *Should America Go to War? The Debate over Foreign
Policy in Chicago, 1939–1941* (Chapel Hill: University of North Carolina
Press, 1989). For a study that focuses on right-wing anti-interventionism,
see Ronald Radosh, *Prophets on the Right: Profiles of Conservative Critics of
American Globalism* (Cybereditions, 2001 [1974]). For one that examines
liberal anti-interventionists, see Daniel W. Aldridge III, "A War for the Col-
ored Races: Anti-Interventionism and the African American Intelligentsia,
1939–1941," *Diplomatic History* 28, no. 3 (2004): 321–52.

4. For this review I have surveyed textbooks used in U.S. history survey courses
at the university and college level and omitted analysis of texts used in U.S.
foreign relations courses, which naturally present a more extensive analysis
of the question. I have used the list of "most used textbooks in U.S." compiled
in 2004 by Daniel J. Cohen for the Center for History and New Media at
George Mason University to guide my selection of texts, omitting concise
editions and adding some titles published since the list was compiled. See
Daniel J. Cohen, "By the Book: Assessing the Place of Textbooks in U.S. Survey Courses," *Journal of American History* 91, no. 4 (March 2005): 1405–15.
For a discussion of the constraints and possibilities in the writing and revis-

ing of survey texts, see Alan Brinkley, "The Challenges and Rewards of Textbook Writing: An Interview with Alan Brinkley," *Journal of American History* 91, no. 4 (March 2005): 1391–97, and Mary Beth Norton, "Reflections of a Longtime Textbook Author; or, History Revised, Revised—and Revised Again," *Journal of American History* 91, no. 4 (March 2005): 1383–90.

5. Jonas, *Isolationism in America*, 3–6.

6. In fact, most texts still use the discredited term "isolationism" in the context of 1939–1941, even when they adopt the more scholarly up-to-date appellations ("independent internationalism" or "unilateralism") for the 1920s and 1930s. See, for instance, Alan Brinkley, *American History*, twelfth ed., vol. II (Boston: McGraw-Hill, 2007).

7. Carol Berkin et al., *Making America*, fourth ed., vol. II (Boston: Houghton Mifflin, 2006), 796–99.

8. Mark C. Carnes and John A. Garraty, *American Destiny*, third ed., vol. II (New York: Pearson Longman, 2008), 746–51; Mark C. Carnes and John A. Garraty, *The American Nation*, twelfth ed., vol. II (New York: Pearson Longman, 2006), 730–36.

9. Gary B. Nash and Julie Roy Jeffrey, *The American People*, seventh ed., vol. II (New York: Pearson Longman, 2006), 828–34.

10. James L. Roark et al., *The American Promise*, third ed., vol. II (Boston: Bedford/St. Martin's, 2005), 914–16.

11. The May 19 radio address is reprinted in Doenecke, *The Battle Against Intervention, 1939–1941*, 126–28. See Wayne S. Cole, *Charles A. Lindbergh and the Battle Against American Intervention in World War II* (New York: Harcourt Brace Jovanovich, 1974), chap. 11; and Doenecke, *Storm on the Horizon*, chap. 7.

12. Cole, *Roosevelt and the Isolationists*, 364.

13. George Brown Tindall and David Emory Shi, *America: A Narrative History*, seventh ed., vol. II (New York: W. W. Norton, 2007), 1078–84.

14. Carnes and Garraty, *American Destiny*, 748; Carnes and Garraty, *American Nation*, 734. They also erroneously state that "after the enactment of lend-lease, aid short of war was no longer seriously debated" (*Destiny*, 751; *Nation*, 736). Anti-interventionists had lost the battle of public opinion by then, but they continued to oppose Roosevelt's policies.

15. Brinkley, *American History*, 728–36.

16. Robert A. Divine et al., *America Past and Present*, seventh ed., vol. II (New

York: Pearson Longman, 2005), 784–85; Robert A. Divine et al., *American Story*, second ed., vol. II (New York: Pearson Longman, 2005), 679–81.

17. David M. Kennedy, Lizabeth Cohen, and Thomas A. Bailey, *The American Pageant*, thirteenth ed., vol. II (Boston: Houghton Mifflin, 2006), 807–20.

18. David Goldfield et al., *The American Journey*, fourth ed., vol. II (New York: Pearson, 2008), 809–16.

19. Mary Beth Norton et al., *A People and a Nation*, seventh ed., vol. II (Boston: Houghton Mifflin, 2005), 724–32.

20. John M. Murrin et al., *Liberty, Equality, Power*, second ed., vol. II (Fort Worth: Harcourt Brace, 1999), 883–84. This, along with a paragraph mentioning America First and Charles Lindbergh, is about all the information this text provides on anti-interventionism. The paragraph immediately following the one cited here focuses on antisemitism and the adoption of a restrictive refugee policy, suggesting a link with anti-interventionism.

21. Schneider, *Should America Go to War?* 153–54; Cole, *Roosevelt and the Isolationists*, 410–11. Roosevelt had an exaggerated fear of "fifth column" infiltration and was willing to violate freedom of expression in order to secure the country's support for aid to the democracies that he considered so essential (this included forwarding anti-interventionist mail received by the White House to the Federal Bureau of Investigation). See Cole, chapter 30.

22. Cole's analysis is focused on the national leadership. See Wayne S. Cole, *America First: The Battle Against Intervention, 1940–41* (Madison: University of Wisconsin Press, 1953), 71–79.

23. Paul S. Boyer et al., *The Enduring Vision*, sixth ed., vol. II (Boston: Houghton Mifflin, 2008), 772.

24. John Mack Faragher et al., *Out of Many*, fifth ed., vol. II (Upper Saddle River, N.J.: Pearson Prentice Hall, 2006), 746–47.

25. www.pbs.org/wgbh/amex/lindbergh/filmmore/reference/primary/desmoinesspeech.html.

26. Cole, *America First*, 131; Jonas, *Isolationism in America*, 255; and Schneider, *Should America Go to War?* 210. See also Cole, *Charles A. Lindbergh and the Battle Against American Intervention*, 171–72; Walter L. Hixson, *Charles A. Lindbergh: Lone Eagle*, ed. Mark C. Carnes, third ed., Library of American Biography (New York: Pearson, 2007), 121–23; and A. Scott Berg, *Lindbergh* (New York: G. P. Putnam's Sons, 1998), 385–86, 393, and 425–27.

27. Cole, *America First*, 132–41; Cole, *Roosevelt and the Isolationists*, 380.
28. Jacqueline Jones et al., *Created Equal*, second ed., vol. II (New York: Pearson Longman, 2006), 777.
29. Eric Foner, *Give Me Liberty!* Seagull ed., vol. II (New York: W. W. Norton, 2006), 740–43; the reference to national security is on p. 742: "Roosevelt viewed Hitler as a mad gangster whose victories posed a direct threat to the United States."

3: "THE GOOD WAR"

1. *The Greatest Generation* (New York: Random House, 1998), 3, 7.
2. *Band of Brothers: E Company, 506th Regiment, 101st Airborne. From Normandy to Hitler's Eagle's Nest* (New York: Simon & Schuster, 2001 [1992]), 13; *Citizen Soldiers: The U.S. Army from the Normandy Beaches to the Bulge to the Surrender of Germany, June 7, 1944–May 7, 1945* (New York: Simon & Schuster, 1997), 14; and *The Good Fight: How World War II Was Won* (New York: Atheneum, 2001), 4. For an excellent review of *The Good Fight* that places the book in the context of Ambrose's overall interpretation, see Benjamin Schwarz, "The Real War," *The Atlantic*, June 2001, www.theatlantic.com/doc/200106/schwarz.
3. *Citizen*, 14 ("speak with"); on the veterans' participation in the writing of *Band of Brothers*, see "Acknowledgments and Sources," 312.
4. Paul Fussell, *Wartime: Understanding and Behavior in the Second World War* (New York: Oxford University Press, 1989), 142. Chapter 10 is especially relevant to the issues raised by Sledge (on the importance of patriotic sentiment for the soldiers). E. B. Sledge, *With the Old Breed at Peleliu and Okinawa* (New York: Oxford University Press, 1981). His comments to Terkel can be found in Studs Terkel, *"The Good War": An Oral History of World War Two* (New York: Pantheon Books, 1984), 59–60, and at www.studsterkel.org/gwar.php ("We were patriots" is from the interview posted on this website). See also historian Howard Zinn's account of his enthusiastic joining of the U.S. Army Air Force in 1943 and his later questioning of "the motives, the conduct, and the consequences of that crusade." *Just War* (Milano, Italy: Charta, 2005), 31, and *Declarations of Independence: Cross-Examining American Ideology* (New York: HarperPerennial, 1990), 80.
5. Richard Polenberg, "The Good War? A Reappraisal of How World War II

Affected American Society," *The Virginia Magazine of History and Biography* 100, no. 3 (July 1992): 322. Michael Adams, *The Best War Ever: America and World War II* (Baltimore: Johns Hopkins University Press, 1994), xiv. For an overview of historians' questioning of the Good War and a historical summary of how the idea evolved in the postwar period, see John W. Jeffries, *Wartime America: The World War II Home Front* (Chicago: Ivan R. Dee, 1996), 8-13.

6. Samuel Hynes, "Personal Narratives and Commemoration," in *War and Remembrance in the Twentieth Century*, Jay Winter and Emmanuel Sivan, eds. (Cambridge: Cambridge University Press, 1999), 207.

7. Nicholson Baker, *Human Smoke: The Beginnings of World War II, the End of Civilization* (New York: Simon & Schuster, 2008), 1 (Nobel), 474 (Afterword). Pickett of the American Friends Service Committee appears for the first time in the book when he traveled to Germany to explore ways of assisting the emigration of persecuted Jews in May 1934 (p. 49).

8. See Colm Tóibín, "Their Vilest Hour," NYTimes.com, March 23, 2008. For prepublication coverage that explains Baker's methodologies and the questions that led him to the book, see Charles McGrath, "A Debunker on the Road to World War II," NYTimes.com, March 4, 2008. I disagree with McGrath's statement that "*Human Smoke* deliberately has no argument."

9. Churchill's commitment to "total war" is traced back to May 1940, when the British war cabinet decided to bomb the Ruhr Valley—before the German blitz on London (p. 181). The killing of German civilians becomes, from then on, a constant theme in Baker's narrative (e.g., pp. 183, 185, 226-27, 238, 250, 260, 327, 334, 381, 388). "Compared with the mass raids that began two years later [in 1942], the damage that the Royal Air Force's bombers did was minuscule and unsustained, but it didn't feel that way to German civilians" (p. 207). Churchill's support for chemical weaponry is mentioned on p. 224.

10. Gandhi's radicalism is at times arresting: "If Hitler and Mussolini chose to overrun England [Gandhi wrote in an open letter to the people of England on July 3, 1940], [they should] let them. 'If these gentlemen choose to occupy your homes, you will vacate them. If they do not give you free passage out, you will allow yourself, man, woman and child, to be slaughtered, but you will refuse to owe allegiance to them.' This method, Gandhi said, had had considerable success in India" (Baker, *Human Smoke*, 206). Yet perhaps

it was not as unreasonable as it first appeared: "No doubt the determination is natural and worthy of the best British tradition," Gandhi wrote again a few days later (in reply to the reply his open letter had generated). "Nevertheless the awful slaughter that the determination involves should induce a search for a better and braver way to achieve the end" (p. 210).

11. Baker, *Human Smoke*, 204. That the British government's willingness to make peace would allow Jews to move to Madagascar is also suggested on pp. 207, 233, and 245. The shift from emigration to the policy of mass extermination ("the final solution") is noted on pp. 371 and 430.

12. On efforts (mostly frustrated) to send food relief to populations under Nazi control, see Baker, *Human Smoke*, 220, 223, 236, 246, 259, 262, 306, 353, 355, 411, and 439.

## PART II: TO "CREATE A WILL TO WIN"

1. On Marshall's and Osborn's directives, see James J. Lorence, *Screening America: United States History Through Film Since 1900* (New York: Pearson, 2006), 98.

## 4: "IT'S EVERYBODY'S JOB"

1. Thomas Doherty, *Projections of War: Hollywood, American Culture and World War II* (New York: Columbia University Press, 1993), 70–75, 79. David Culbert, " 'Why We Fight': Social Engineering for a Democratic Society at War," in *Film and Radio Propaganda in World War II*, K.R.M. Short, ed. (London: Croom Helm, 1983); Kathleen M. German, "Frank Capra's *Why We Fight* Series and the American Audience," *Western Journal of Speech Communication* 54 (Spring 1990): 244; and Richard Dyer MacCann, "World War II: Armed Forces Documentary," in *Nonfiction Film: Theory and Criticism*, ed. Richard Meran Barsam (New York: Dutton, 1976).

2. Eric Smoodin, *Animating Culture: Hollywood Cartoons from the Sound Era* (New Brunswick, N.J.: Rutgers University Press, 1993), 71–95; the quote is on p. 73. Benjamin L. Alpers, "This Is the Army: Imagining a Democratic Military in World War II," *Journal of American History* 85, no. 1 (June 1998): 129–63.

3. John Philip Falter, *This World Cannot Exist Half Slave and Half Free* (Wash-

ington, D.C.: U.S. Government Printing Office, 1942). A digital image of this poster can be viewed at the University of North Texas Digital Library, digital.library.unt.edu/ark:/67531/metadc483. Ben Shahn, *This Is Nazi Brutality* (Washington, D.C.: U.S. Government Printing Office, 1942). Available in the University of Minnesota Libraries' War Posters Collection. See snuffy.lib.umn.edu/image/srch/bin/Dispatcher?mode=600&id=mpw00499.

4. *"We'll Have Lots to Eat This Winter, Won't We Mother?"* (Washington, D.C.: U.S. Government Printing Office, 1943). See digital.library.unt.edu/ark:/67531/metadc556.

5. Allan M. Winkler, *The Politics of Propaganda: The Office of War Information, 1942–1945* (New Haven, Conn.: Yale University Press, 1978), 13 ("honest facts"), 64–65 (resignation letters); Frank W. Fox, *Madison Avenue Goes to War: The Strange Military Career of American Advertising, 1941–1945* (Provo, Utah: Brigham Young University Press, 1975), 52 ("In shock"). See also John Morton Blum, *V Was for Victory: Politics and American Culture During World War II* (New York: Harcourt Brace Jovanovich, 1976), 15–45, and Sydney Weinberg, "What to Tell America: The Writers' Quarrel in the Office of War Information," *Journal of American History* 55, no. 1 (June 1968): 73–89.

6. William L. Bird, Jr., and Harry R. Rubenstein, *Design for Victory: World War II Posters on the American Home Front* (New York: Princeton Architectural Press, 1998), 11–12. In addition to the online collections used in this chapter, several published collections of posters are available, including Bird's and Rubenstein's and Michael E. Moss, *Posters for Victory: The American Home Front and World War II* (West Point, N.Y.: United States Military Academy, 1978).

7. This point has been made by others. See, for instance, George H. Roeder, Jr., *The Censored War: American Visual Experience During World War Two* (New Haven, Conn.: Yale University Press, 1993), 43: "The theme propagandists promoted most insistently was that everyone had a part to play." McClelland Barclay, *Defend American Freedom: It's Everybody's Job* (New York: National Association of Manufacturers, 1942). See digital.library .unt.edu/ark:/67531/metadc611.

8. U.S. Department of the Treasury, *We Can . . . We Will . . . We Must!* (Washington, D.C.: U.S. Government Printing Office, 1942). See digital.library.unt .edu/ark:/67531/metadc415. Lawrence R. Samuel, *Pledging Allegiance: Ameri-*

*can Identity and the Bond Drive of World War II* (Washington, D.C.: Smithsonian Institution Press, 1997), 51. For the number of posters produced, see Bird and Rubenstein, *Design for Victory*, 9.

9. Roeder, *Censored War*, 81. On the complex history of Joe Rosenthal's famous photograph, see Karal Ann Marling and John Wetenhall, *Iwo Jima: Monuments, Memories, and the American Hero* (Cambridge, Mass.: Harvard University Press, 1991) and Alpers, "This Is the Army," 141–42. *Now All Together* (Washington, D.C.: U.S. Government Printing Office, 1945) can be viewed at digital.library.unt.edu/ark:/67531/metadc578.

10. Alpers also notes that "the multiethnic and multiregional unit became a central representation of the military" (p. 143). Courtney Allen, *Together We Win* (Washington, D.C.: U.S. Government Printing Office, 1943), at snuffy .lib.umn.edu/image/srch/bin/Dispatcher?mode=600&id=mpw00044; *United We Win* (Washington, D.C.: U.S. Government Printing Office, 1943), Northwestern University Library, World War II Poster Collection at www.library.northwestern.edu/govinfo/collections/wwii-posters/. *Every Man, Woman and Child Is a Partner* (Washington, D.C.: U.S. Government Printing Office, 1942), digital.library.unt.edu/ark:/67531/metadc211.

11. See *Don't Let That Shadow Touch Them* (Washington, D.C.: U.S. Government Printing Office, 1942), digital.library.unt.edu/ark:/67531/metadc205; *Ours—to Fight For: Freedom from Want* (Washington, D.C.: U.S. Government Printing Office, 1943), digital.library.unt.edu/ark:/67531/metadc554; *Ours— to Fight For: Freedom from Fear* (Washington, D.C.: U.S. Government Printing Office, 1943), digital.library.unt.edu/ark:/67531/metadc372; Fox, *Madison Avenue Goes to War*; Robert B. Westbrook, *Why We Fought: Forging American Obligations in World War II* (Washington, D.C.: Smithsonian Books, 2004), especially chapters 2 and 3.

12. McClelland Barclay, *"Arise Americans": Your Country and Your Liberty Are in Grave Danger* (Washington, D.C.: U.S. Navy Recruiting Bureau, 1941), digital.library.unt.edu/ark:/67531/metadc612; *The U.S. Marines Want You* (ca. 1942), snuffy.lib.umn.edu/image/srch/bin/Dispatcher?mode=600&id= msp04443; *Are You Doing All You Can?* (1942), snuffy.lib.umn.edu/image/ srch/bin/Dispatcher?mode=600&id=msp02215.

13. Samuel, *Pledging Allegiance*, describes organized labor's support for the bond drives in chapter 4; *I'm No Millionaire, But . . .* is reproduced in Bird and Rubenstein, *Design for Victory* (p. 21), along with the revised version used in the 1942 campaign. *Wanted—Fighting Dollars* (Washington, D.C.:

U.S. Government Printing Office, 1942) can also be found at digital.library
.unt.edu/ark:/67531/metadc242. For another poster displaying the workers'
cap, see one produced by GM's Pontiac Motor Division, *Come On Gang!
We're Building Arms for Victory!* in *Design for Victory* (p. 10), also available
at americanhistory.si.edu/victory/victory1.htm.

14. Anton Bruehl, *Free Labor Will Win* (Washington, D.C.: U.S. Government
Printing Office, 1942), snuffy.lib.umn.edu/image/srch/bin/Dispatcher?
mode=600&id=mpw00021; Willmarths, *Let's All Get "Steamed Up"* (n.d.),
snuffy.lib.umn.edu/image/srch/bin/Dispatcher?mode=600&id=msp02309;
*American Labor . . . Producing for Attack* (Washington, D.C.: U.S.
Government Printing Office, 1943), snuffy.lib.umn.edu/image/srch/bin/
Dispatcher?mode=600&id=msp02255; Garrett W. Price, *Pour It On!*
(Washington, D.C.: U.S. Government Printing Office, 1942), snuffy.lib
.umn.edu/image/srch/bin/Dispatcher?mode=600&id=mpw00036; McClelland Barclay, *Man the Guns* (1942), is available electronically at www
.history.navy.mil/ac/artist/b/barclay/barclay%202.html; *Dish It Out with
the Navy!* (Washington, D.C.: U.S. Navy Recruiting Bureau, 1942), digital
.library.unt.edu/ark:/67531/metadc610.

15. James J. Kimble argues that this "conflation of the worlds of civilians and
soldiers" was central to the early war bond campaigns. See *Mobilizing the
Home Front: War Bonds and Domestic Propaganda* (College Station: Texas
A&M University Press, 2006), 46–53. See also Samuel, *Pledging Allegiance*,
50. Henry Koerner, *Save Waste Fats for Explosives* (Washington, D.C.: U.S.
Government Printing Office, 1943), snuffy.lib.umn.edu/image/srch/bin/
Dispatcher?mode=600&id=msp02711; *Men Working Together!* (Washington,
D.C.: U.S. Government Printing Office, 1942), digital.library.unt.edu/ark:/
67531/metadc478; *Let's All Pull Together!* (General Motors Corp., n.d.),
snuffy.lib.umn.edu/image/srch/bin/Dispatcher?mode=600&id=msp00096.

16. Kimble, *Mobilizing the Home Front*, 67 ("the only way"), 76 ("thrust home");
Roeder, *The Censored War*.

17. Frederic Stanley, *What Did You Do Today . . . for Freedom?* (Washington,
D.C.: U.S. Government Printing Office, 1943), www.library.northwestern
.edu/govinfo/collections/wwii-posters/; John Philip Falter, *A Strange Sort
of Prayer* (n.d.), snuffy.lib.umn.edu/image/srch/bin/Dispatcher?mode=
600&id=mpw00075.

18. Kimble, *Mobilizing the Home Front*, 54–55 ("wary of attempts"), 88–94 (for
representations of the enemy in the Treasury's campaigns of 1944 and 1945).

John W. Dower, *War Without Mercy: Race and Power in the Pacific War* (New York: Pantheon Books, 1986).

19. Mary Poovey, *Uneven Development: The Ideological Work of Gender in Mid-Victorian England* (Chicago: University of Chicago Press, 1988), 2–4.

## 5: A MATTER OF PRIVATE OBLIGATIONS?

1. Robert B. Westbrook, *Why We Fought: Forging American Obligations in World War II* (Washington, D.C.: Smithsonian Books, 2004). Chapters 2 and 3 are slightly revised versions of "Fighting for the American Family: Private Interests and Political Obligation in World War II," in *The Power of Culture: Critical Essays in American History*, eds. Richard Wightman Fox and T. J. Jackson Lears (Chicago: University of Chicago Press, 1993), 195–221, and "'I Want a Girl, Just Like the Girl That Married Harry James': American Women and the Problem of Political Obligation in World War II," *American Quarterly* 42 (1990): 587–614. The essays are most often cited and used in their original versions.

2. Westbrook, *Why We Fought*, 13.

3. Ibid., 16.

4. Ibid., 8.

5. Ibid., 17.

6. Michael Walzer, *Obligations: Essays on Disobedience, War, and Citizenship* (Cambridge, Mass.: Harvard University Press, 1970), 82.

7. Ibid., 89.

8. Westbrook, *Why We Fought*, 44. Walzer's influence and theory are explained at length in the introduction to the originally published essays. *Why We Fought* presents a condensed version.

9. Frank W. Fox, *Madison Avenue Goes to War* (Provo, Utah: Brigham Young University Press, 1975), 59 ("tactic"), 11 ("self-consciously came"), 60 ("suffused"), 69 ("We fight"). Allan M. Winkler, *The Politics of Propaganda* (New Haven, Conn.: Yale University Press, 1978).

10. Westbrook, *Why We Fought*, 51.

11. Ibid., 50–55.

12. Ibid., 46.

13. Ibid., 48–50. On Rockwell's painting of the Four Freedoms and the paintings' use in the bond drive of April–May 1943, see Stuart and James McCabe

Murray, *Norman Rockwell's Four Freedoms: Images That Inspire a Nation* (Stockbridge, Mass.: Berkshire House Publishers, 1993).

14. Westbrook, *Why We Fought,* 73.

15. Ibid., 78, 80.

16. Ibid., 18.

17. Rogers M. Smith, *Civic Ideals: Conflicting Visions of Citizenship in U.S. History* (New Haven, Conn.: Yale University Press, 1997). The works by Smith that Westbrook cites are articles published earlier (see Westbrook, 127, n. 6). John Bodnar, ed., *Bonds of Affection: Americans Define Their Patriotism* (Princeton, N.J.: Princeton University Press, 1996).

18. Westbrook, *Why We Fought*, 58.

19. Ibid., 33.

20. Ibid., 59.

21. Ibid.

22. Ibid., 62. This point is reinforced in the book's introduction (p. 9), in which *Freedom of Speech* is characterized as presenting an "exceptional, nonliberal argument."

23. A criticism of this type of dual analysis has been presented by Gary Gerstle in *American Crucible: Race and Nation in the Twentieth Century* (Princeton, N.J.: Princeton University Press, 2001), 198. "There can be no doubt that individual and familial well-being loomed large in the minds of many Americans. But it seems wrong to divorce the personal from the national in so mechanical a way, as though individuals make a clear-cut decision to embrace one or the other. In America, in particular, the promise of prosperity was integral to the civic nationalist ideal."

### 6: GENDERED PATRIOTS

1. Linda Kerber, *No Constitutional Right to Be Ladies: Women and the Obligations of Citizenship* (New York: Hill and Wang, 1998). The gendered assumptions that shape American citizenship are common to Western liberal thought, as the influential work of Carole Pateman has shown. See her *Sexual Contract* (Stanford: Stanford University Press, 1988). For a study of the language of sacrifice that points to dynamics of class relations, see Mark H. Leff, "The Politics of Sacrifice on the American Home Front in World War II," *Journal of American History* 77, no. 4 (March 1991): 1296–318.

2. As described by George Q. Flynn, in *The Mess in Washington: Manpower Mobilization in World War II* (Westport, Conn.: Greenwood Press, 1979), military and political leaders were not concerned about female recruitment until the middle of 1943, when the ranks of the unemployed were depleted and a need for more soldiers was acutely felt (pp. 40, 175). See also Alice Kessler-Harris, *Out to Work: A History of Wage-Earning Women in the United States* (New York: Oxford University Press, 1982), 275–78. The number of women employed jumped from around 10 million in 1940 to a peak of 19 million in 1944–1945; their percentage of the total U.S. workforce rose from 24 percent to about 33 percent. The employers' early reluctance to employ women is described by Karen Anderson, *Wartime Women: Sex Roles, Family Relations, and the Status of Women During World War II* (Westport, Conn: Greenwood Press, 1981), 23–26. On women's motivations, see 28. See also Lynn Y. Weiner, *From Working Girl to Working Mother: The Female Labor Force in the United States, 1820–1980* (Chapel Hill, N.C.: University of North Carolina Press, 1985).

3. Maureen Honey, *Creating Rosie the Riveter: Class, Gender, and Propaganda During World War II* (Amherst, Mass.: University of Massachusetts Press, 1984), 51, 131. Honey analyzed fiction and advertising in two major magazines: *The Saturday Evening Post*, which had a middle-class readership, featured the themes summarized here. The other magazine she analyzed, *True Story*, had a working-class audience and featured a similar emphasis on self-sacrifice. Jane Marcellus has analyzed the portrayal of female workers in the employee magazine published by Henry J. Kaiser's Oregon Shipbuilding Corporation, one of the largest employers of women workers. Emphasizing the oddity and sexuality of women workers, Marcellus concludes, helped Kaiser reconcile the conflicting pressures of depicting the female workers in a positive light and refraining from encouraging socially disruptive trends. See "Bo's'n's Whistle: Representing 'Rosie the Riveter' on the Job," *American Journalism* 22, no. 2 (Spring 2005): 83–108. See also Melissa Dabakis, "Gendered Labor: Norman Rockwell's *Rosie the Riveter* and the Discourses of Wartime Womanhood," in Barbara Melosh, ed., *Gender and American History Since 1890* (New York: Routledge, 1993), 182–204. See also Leila J. Rupp, *Mobilizing Women for War: German and American Propaganda, 1939–1945* (Princeton, N.J.: Princeton University Press, 1978).

4. Susan M. Hartmann, "Prescriptions for Penelope: Literature on Women's Obligations to Returning World War II Veterans," *Women's Studies* 5 (1978): 236.

5. A good description of the rationing system is provided in Richard R. Lingeman, *Don't You Know There's a War On? The American Home Front, 1941–1945* (New York: Capricorn Books, 1976 [1970]), chapter 7. The newspaper information is quoted on pp. 256–57. I borrow the term "Wartime Homemaker" from Amy Bentley, *Eating for Victory: Food Rationing and the Politics of Domesticity* (Urbana: University of Illinois Press, 1998), 31. She examines the decentralized model adopted by the OPA on pp. 17, 28–29, 37 and the "social engineering" model employed by the OPA and their reliance on female experts on pp. 24–27. In a brief discussion of the mostly female consumer movement's inability to shape grade labeling policies, Bentley shows the limitations of women's claim to power through their patriotic service as consumers (pp. 50–58). Her interpretation contrasts with that of Meg Jacobs, who attributes substantial political significance to the OPA's mobilization of a vast network of local volunteers. See her "'How About Some Meat?' The Office of Price Administration, Consumption Politics, and State Building from the Bottom Up, 1941–1946," *Journal of American History* 84, no. 3 (December 1997): 910–41, and *Pocketbook Politics: Economic Citizenship in Twentieth-Century America* (Princeton, N. J.: Princeton University Press, 2005), chapter 5. The OPA's decentralized model mirrors that in place to legitimize and administer compulsory military registration (the draft) and manpower allocation. Lingeman notes the effectiveness of the rationing system, which did change patterns of civilians' food consumption: eggs were used as substitutes for beef; margarine consumption increased to make up for the limited supply of butter (pp. 259–65). He also notes a general compliance with both rationing and price control (pp. 269–70). Mei-ling Yang concurs that "rationing won the consent of the majority of Americans" in "Creating the Kitchen Patriot: Media Promotion of Food Rationing and Nutrition Campaigns on the American Home Front During World War II," *American Journalism* 22, no. 3 (Summer 2005): 64. The imperfect regulation of industrial production and manpower allocation is described in Flynn, *The Mess in Washington.*

6. Mei-ling Yang, "Creating the Kitchen Patriot," 59 (italics are in the original). She notes that the gendered notions associated with food consumption

were explicit in public relations material: meat was critical to satisfy the "inner man," while salads and fresh fruits were considered "sissy" (pp. 59–60). On the association of meat with masculinity, see Bentley, *Eating for Victory*, 85–102. The "home front" as a feminized construct is discussed in Bentley, 44.

7. Leisa D. Meyer, *Creating GI Jane: Sexuality and Power in the Women's Army Corps During World War II* (New York: Columbia University Press, 1996), 16. On the nature of women's work in the military, see chapter 4. Meyer notes that the range of occupations open to women in the military, and the opportunity to work in nontraditional fields, was more limited than in the civilian sector (pp. 72–73, 76). As in the civilian labor force, African Americans were typically assigned to menial service work. The Army Air Force was the main outlet for access to nontraditional jobs; see p. 84.

8. A law to authorize women to join the navy, as members of WAVES (Women Accepted for Volunteer Emergency Service), was passed on July 30, 1942. The Marine Corps Women's Reserve was also authorized by Congress in July 1942 and established in February 1943. The U.S. Coast Guard also had a Women's Reserve (SPARS). For an oral history of women who served in, or with, the military as civilians (as nurses or members of the Red Cross), see Olga Gruhzit-Hoyt, *They Also Served: American Women in World War II* (New York: Birch Lane Press, 1995).

9. When WAAC was replaced by WAC, an amendment that would have denied full benefits to women in the military was debated but defeated. Passing it on the ground that women were not in combat positions and therefore not truly deserving of soldiers' benefits proved impossible, given the large number of men who were in noncombat positions in the army (Meyer, *Creating GI Jane*, 46–47). Female army veterans' use of GI Bill benefits is discussed briefly on p. 182.

10. Meyer, *Creating GI Jane*, 52. On women's lack of sexual protection within the army, see pp. 39–42; on accusations of homosexuality within the WAC, see p. 43. On the effort to retain the image of the WAC as a "respectable" organization by maintaining a white and upper-class membership, see pp. 61–68; a quota of 10 percent of the total number of recruits was imposed on the service of African Americans; strict regulation of women's sexual conduct was also put in place (pp. 69–70); see also chapters 5–7.

11. Meyer, *Creating GI Jane*, 53, 59–61.

## COMMENTARY

1. J. H. Hexter, *On Historians: Reappraisals of Some of the Makers of Modern History* (Cambridge, Mass.: Harvard University Press, 1979), 241–42.

## 7: "THEIR WORLD CAN NEVER BE KNOWN TO YOU"

1. Gerald F. Linderman, *The World Within War: America's Combat Experience in World War II* (Cambridge, Mass.: Harvard University Press, 1997), 308. As summarized by the historian Jackson Lears, Whitman "sensed that there was something new about the carnage of modern war, something that resisted literary convention and ultimately language itself." See "Fighting Words," *New Republic* 227, no. 11/12 (September 9 and 16, 2002): 35–41.

2. Mary S. Mander, "American Correspondents During World War II: Common Sense as a View of the World," *American Journalism* 1, no. 1 (Summer 1983): 17–30; John B. Romeiser, ed., *Combat Reporter: Don Whitehead's World War II Diary and Memoirs* (New York: Fordham University Press, 2006), 2. For Ernie Pyle's account of the differences between correspondents who stayed in the comfort of the rear (the majority) and "some of us" who preferred staying at the front, see *Here Is Your War: Story of G.I. Joe* (Lincoln: University of Nebraska Press, 2004), 172. GIs, of course, had their own views of both war and combat correspondents, often failing to see the distinction.

3. John Steinbeck, *Once There Was a War* (New York: Penguin, 2007 [1958]). The quotes are on pp. 123, 125, 131, 128, 162, and 164. For a classic selection of war reportage, see Samuel Hynes in his introduction to *Reporting World War II: American Journalism, 1938–1946* (New York: Library of America, 2001 [1995]).

4. James Tobin, *Ernie Pyle's War: America's Eyewitness to World War II* (New York: Free Press, 2006 [1997]), 53.

5. Quoted in ibid., 67.

6. Ibid., 87–88.

7. David Nichols, ed., *Ernie's War: The Best of Ernie Pyle's World War II Dispatches* (New York: Simon & Schuster, 1986), 97.

8. Tobin, *Ernie Pyle's War*, 149.

9. Nichols, ed., *Ernie's War*, 113.

10. On Mauldin, see Todd DePastino, *Bill Mauldin: A Life Up Front* (New York: W. W. Norton, 2008). "Unshaven, unwashed, unsmiling" is Pyle's characterization of Mauldin's characters; see Nichols, ed., *Ernie's War*, 197–99. Although Mauldin published a book for a civilian readership based on his cartoons (*Up Front*), the cartoons themselves were created for the army publication *Stars and Stripes*.

11. Tobin, *Ernie Pyle's War*, 98, 202. Pyle described such requests in *Here Is Your War*, p. 77, asking his readers not to forget that "unfortunately the world is a big place and our troops were scattered."

12. Richard Collier, *Fighting Words: The Correspondents of World War II* (New York: St. Martin's Press, 1989), 137.

13. Romeiser, ed., *Combat Reporter*, 11.

14. John B. Romeiser, ed., *"Beachhead Don": Reporting the War from the European Theater, 1942–1945* (New York: Fordham University Press, 2004), 21, 27, 19.

15. Tobin, *Ernie Pyle's War*, 243.

16. In *Here Is Your War*, a compilation of his North Africa dispatches published in October 1943, Pyle used the word "visiting" to describe his first encounter with a frontline outfit (p. 115). In the original dispatch, written in February, Pyle had used the phrase "living with a front-line outfit" (Nichols, ed., *Ernie's War*, 79). This change of wording suggests that, by the time Pyle revised his dispatches for publication during a brief return to the United States, he had a more sophisticated—or perhaps more ambiguous—understanding of his relationship to the troops. Bill Mauldin, although respected by frontline troops, would also be reminded of his outsider status by a reader of *Stars and Stripes* after his cartoons started appearing under the title of "Up Front . . . with Mauldin" in December 1943. Mauldin responded by altering the title to "Up Front . . . by Mauldin" (DePastino, 124–25). The letter is reproduced in Todd DePastino, ed., *Willie and Joe: The WWII Years*, vol. II (Seattle: Fantagraphics Books, 2008), 42. For a similar sentiment about Whitehead, see Command Sergeant Major Benjamin Franklin, Sixteenth Regiment, First Infantry Division, "Afterword," Romeiser, ed., *Combat Reporter*, 207–208. On the combat soldiers' views of reporters, including the most loved ones, see Tobin, *Ernie Pyle's War*, 77–78.

17. Tobin, *Ernie Pyle's War*, 79; Pyle, *Here Is Your War*, 173.

18. Nichols, ed., *Ernie's War*, 103–104; Pyle, *Here Is Your War*, 195–96; Tobin, *Ernie Pyle's War*, 88–89.

19. Pyle, *Here Is Your War*, 244.

20. Nichols, ed., *Ernie's War*, 270–71.

21. Romeiser, ed., *Beachhead Don*, 69, 129. Pyle also admonished "you people at home" for assuming that the landings in France suggested that the European campaign would soon be over: "Folks newly arrived from America say that you people at home are grave and eager about this . . . But they say also that you are giving the landings themselves an importance out of proportion to what must follow before the war can end." The tone was conciliatory, but direct nevertheless: "It is natural for you to feel that, and nobody is blaming you. But I thought maybe in this column I could help your understanding of things if we sort of charted this European campaign. This is not an attempt to predict—it is just an effort to clarify" (Nichols, ed., *Ernie's War*, 286–87).

22. Nichols, ed., *Ernie's War*, 81–83; Pyle, *Here Is Your War*, 123–26, 200; Nichols, ed., *Ernie's War*, 113.

23. Nichols, ed., *Ernie's War*, 153, 172, 330.

24. Ibid., 419.

### 8: WRITING HOME: INTIMATE CONVERSATIONS ABOUT WAR

1. Minoru Masuda, *Letters from the 442nd: The World War II Correspondence of a Japanese American Medic,* ed. Hana Masuda and Dianne Bridgman (Seattle: University of Washington Press, 2008), 7.

2. Monica Sone offers a firsthand account of the "clap of thunder" that struck the Minidoka internees in 1943: Monica Sone, *Nisei Daughter* (Seattle: University of Washington Press, 1979 [1953]), 198–201. Her family, also from Seattle, followed a path similar to that of the Masudas through Camp Harmony and Minidoka. Her brother, although incensed by their treatment, also volunteered, but he failed the medical examination. For a general survey of the incarceration of Japanese Americans, see Roger Daniels, *Prisoners Without Trial: Japanese Americans in World War II* (New York: Hill and Wang, 1993). For a visual account of their experience, consult Linda Gordon and Gary Y. Okihiro, eds., *Impounded: Dorothea Lange and the Censored Images of Japanese American Internment* (New York: W. W. Norton, 2006). Greg Robinson examines the policy from the point of view of President Roosevelt in *By Order of the President: FDR and the Internment of Japanese Americans* (Cambridge, Mass.: Harvard University Press, 2001).

On Nisei military service, see Masayo Umezawa Duus, *Unlikely Liberators: The Men of the 100th and 442nd*, trans. Peter Duus (Honolulu: University of Hawaii Press, 1987) and Thelma Chang, *"I Can Never Forget": Men of the 100th/442nd* (Honolulu: Sigi Productions, 1991). On the draft resisters, see Eric Muller, *Free to Die for Their Country: The Story of the Japanese American Draft Resisters in World War II* (Chicago: University of Chicago Press, 2001). For a fascinating analysis of the internees' complex responses to their internment and demand for military service, which included voluntary renunciation of citizenship, see Mae M. Ngai, *Impossible Subjects: Illegal Aliens and the Making of Modern America* (Princeton, N.J.: Princeton University Press, 2004), chapter 5.

3. Masuda, *Letters from the 442nd*, 6, 7.

4. The literature on World War II pacifism is vast. For an analysis of pacifist arguments against war, and particularly against the war against Hitler, see Cynthia Eller, *Conscientious Objectors and the Second World War: Moral and Religious Arguments in Support of Pacifism* (New York: Praeger, 1991). For personal accounts by conscientious objectors, see Heather T. Frazer and John O'Sullivan, *"We Have Just Begun to Not Fight": An Oral History of Conscientious Objectors in Civilian Public Service During World War II* (New York: Twayne Publishers, 1996). See also *The Good War and Those Who Refused to Fight It*, DVD, directed by Judith Ehrlich and Rich Tejada-Flores (Berkeley, Calif: Paradigm Productions, 2000), and the accompanying PBS website, www.pbs.org/itvs/thegoodwar/.

5. The importance of letters to soldiers' morale is well documented. In World War II, extraordinary public and private effort was devoted to ensuring speedy delivery of voluminous mailbags. The importance, and mechanisms, of World War II mail are documented in Judy Barrett Litoff and David C. Smith, " 'Will He Get My Letter?' Popular Portrayals of Mail and Morale During World War II," *Journal of Popular Culture* 23, no. 4 (Spring 1990): 21–43; and Thomas Wildenberg, "You've Got V-Mail," *Naval History* 19, no. 3 (2005): 23–25.

6. See his *Radical Pacifism: The War Resisters League and Gandhian Nonviolence in America, 1915–1963* (Syracuse, N.Y.: Syracuse University Press, 2003).

7. Scott H. Bennett, ed., *Army GI, Pacifist CO: The World War II Letters of Frank and Albert Dietrich* (Bronx, N.Y.: Fordham University Press, 2005), 5–6.

8. Ibid., 99, 286, 293.

9. Ibid., 53.

10. Ibid., 78.

11. Ibid., 79.

12. Ibid., 47.

13. Ibid., 51. See also 60.

14. Ibid., 74.

15. As Frazer and O'Sullivan noted, in contrast with the Mennonites and Brethren, whose acceptance of military service "would have been 'frowned on'" by their families and churches, opting for a CO position required for many "a great deal of soul searching." *"We Have Just Begun to Not Fight,"* xix.

16. Bennett, ed., *Army GI*, 56.

17. Ibid., 94.

18. Ibid., 97–98.

19. Ibid., 100.

20. Ibid., 138–39.

21. Ibid., 131. Albert had written that he was considering volunteering for the Smoke Jumpers because "it offers a demonstration that the pacifist is not a C.O. simply to avoid risking his own neck" (p. 114).

22. Ibid., 83. Frank's impression was that their long discussion "was intelligent" and the attitudes of these relatives "quite tolerant" (p. 83). This seems to summarize their immediate family's position as well. As Albert wrote on a postcard: "I believe Dad is now 100% behind me, well not quite 100%, but he accepts my position and knows that there is no use trying to change me" (p. 86).

23. Bennett, ed., *Army GI*, 57.

24. Ibid., 63.

25. Ibid., 66.

26. Ibid., 288–89.

27. Ibid., 253 (my emphasis).

28. Ibid., 293.

29. Eller, *Conscientious Objectors*, 34.

30. Bennett, ed., *Army GI*, 77.

31. Ibid., 80.

32. Ibid., 170, 174.

33. Ibid., 193–94, 228–31.

34. Ibid., 135.

35. Ibid., 140.

36. Ibid., 101.

37. Ibid., 296.

38. Masuda, *Letters from the 442nd*, 8.

39. Ibid., 16.

40. Ibid., 249. Based on a comment he made on October 9, 1945, he seemed to have also kept in very irregular contact with his older brother and sister-in-law, Sat and Rose: "You see I just yesterday heard from [them] and I hastened to write because I'd neglected them, too" (p. 253). On July 25, 1945, he reported receiving a letter from his sister, Nay, who was resettling on a poultry farm in Portland, Oregon (p. 241). His hesitant command of Japanese is suggested in this comment: "I just wrote your mother in my hopeless Japanese—there's a remote possibility that she may get the drift; I wrote it on that strength" (p. 77).

41. Ibid., 77, 120.

42. Ibid., 86.

43. Ibid., 141–42.

44. Ibid., 260.

45. Ibid., 81.

46. Ibid., 43 (emphasis in original). On June 26, 1945, the first anniversary of his unit's first engagement, he did write—if not "all" about it—a long and emotional account of that first day. Composed in an uninterrupted stream of consciousness—four printed pages with no paragraph breaks—the letter described in detail the "rude awakening" that awaited the green troops, the "abject terror . . . in those first moments," the hours the medics spent giving the men plasma under constant shelling, and finally their evacuation of the wounded under cover of darkness. "I got rather carried away in this relating, so you'll excuse it," he concluded his story before moving on to "pleasanter subjects," but "now that it's all over here I thought maybe I'd tell you a story, for now you won't worry about it, and the date egged me on."

47. Ibid., 45.

48. Ibid., 49–50.

49. Ibid., 51.

50. The unit was then attached to the Seventh Army; they fought in the battles of Bruyères and Biffontaine on October 15–22, 1944. On October 26–31, the unit was sent to rescue the "Lost Battalion." Thelma Chang notes: "Within

a month of fighting . . . the 100th/442nd lost about two-thirds of its men . . . For the Lost Battalion ordeal alone, casualties suffered by the Japanese Americans [more than 800] were more than four times the number of men rescued [211]." Chang, *"I Can Never Forget,"* 52–60.

51. Masuda, *Letters from the 442nd*, 104.

52. Ibid., 117–18.

53. Ibid., 124.

54. Ibid., 10. His identification with the typical American GI is illustrated by his association with the heroes of Bill Mauldin's cartoons, which he sent to Hana with the comment "We can recall in them our own experiences" (p. 67). He also personally recruited the support of Ernie Pyle, the self-proclaimed champion of "the God-damned infantry," in his protest against the delay in granting medics combat pay (pp. 126, 155, 245).

55. Ibid., 200.

56. Ibid., 120.

57. Ibid., 89.

58. Ibid., 74.

59. Ibid., 35.

60. Ibid., 228.

61. Ibid., 228–29.

62. Ibid., 109.

63. Ibid., 242.

64. The 442nd Regimental Combat Team was the most decorated unit for its size and length of service, and their exploits were heavily publicized at home. Press coverage of the Nisei troops' success and casualty rates was carefully managed by the army, the 442nd itself, the Japanese-American Citizens League, and the War Relocation Authority. See Patricia A. Curtin, "Press Coverage of the 442nd Regimental Combat Team (Separate-Nisei): A Case Study in Agenda Building," *American Journalism* 12, no. 3 (Summer 1995): 225–41.

65. Masuda, *Letters from the 442nd*, 68–69.

66. Ibid., 245.

67. Ibid., 261–65.

68. Ibid., 5.

69. Diane C. Fujino, *Heartbeat of Struggle: The Revolutionary Life of Yuri Kochiyama* (Minneapolis: University of Minnesota Press, 2005), 6.

70. Masuda, *Letters from the 442nd*, 7.

71. Ibid., 273.
72. Ngai, *Impossible Subjects*, 200.

## 9: IDENTITIES

1. Gary Gerstle, *American Crucible: Race and Nation in the Twentieth Century* (Princeton, N.J.: Princeton University Press, 2001), introduction and chapter 5. This pivotal point in his analysis—the broadened definition of whiteness and the racial exclusions reinforced by military policies and cultural representations—is developed on pp. 202–10. The section based on combatants' memoirs (pp. 220–27) also supports his argument. The lasting impact of wartime racial segregation is discussed on pp. 231–37. The quotes are from pp. 204 ("a unit"), 205 ("Thus battle itself"), and 233 ("The exclusion of blacks"). On representations of the multiethnic combat unit, see also Benjamin L. Alpers, "This Is the Army: Imagining a Democratic Military in World War II," *Journal of American History* 85, no. 1 (June 1998): 143–47. Deborah Dash Moore notes that regional identities typically indicate ethnic differentiation in the war movies, which include "at least one person each from Texas, the Midwest, and Brooklyn. Brooklyn represented a typical urban community. Someone from Brooklyn was surely a white ethnic, which usually meant either a Catholic or a Jew." See her *GI Jews: How World War II Changed a Generation* (Cambridge, Mass.: Belknap Press of Harvard University Press, 2004), 59–60.
2. Leonard Dinnerstein, *Anti-Semitism in America* (New York: Oxford University Press, 1994). Dinnerstein reports that 45 percent of high school respondents to a poll in November 1942 chose Jews as their last choice as a roommate; only African Americans scored higher, with 78 percent of respondents identifying them as undesirable roommates (131). On the lifting of quotas after the war, see p. 158. Dinnerstein also discusses antisemitism in the armed forces on pp. 137–42. On rising antisemitism, employment discrimination, and college quotas facing the two million Jews who lived in New York City, see Beth S. Wenger, *New York Jews and the Great Depression: Uncertain Promise* (New York: Syracuse University Press, 1999).
3. Deborah Dash Moore, "Jewish GIs and the Creation of the Judeo-Christian Tradition," *Religion and American Culture* 8, no. 1 (Winter 1998): 34–35. On the development of the Judeo-Christian tradition, see also her *GI Jews*, 10.

4. Moore, "Jewish GIs." The quotes are from pp. 33 ("equal to" and "the democratic"), 36 ("Jews and Christians"), and 37 ("My Judaism").

5. Moore, *GI Jews*, 26–27, 81, 165–71.

6. "Most Americans . . . ," ibid., 25. Moore qualifies this statement somewhat by noting that this ideological awareness was especially strong among older men who remembered the anti-Jewish violence of the late 1930s; those who were politically aware also knew about the Final Solution, which became public knowledge in November 1942 (p. 44). "Their war" is on p. 48. Moore also notes that the Pacific theater held no meaning for Jewish GIs (pp. 90–93). In contrast, those who fought in Europe felt a concrete sense of affinity, sometimes reinforced by personal encounters, with the Jewish victims of fascism (pp. 104–17; this question is further developed on pp. 167–68 and 193). Moments, such as the 1944 celebration of the Jewish New Year—the first Rosh Hashanah openly observed since the German occupation of the Continent four years earlier—held particular importance in consolidating the special meaning that the war had for Jews (pp. 209–10). Accounts of Jewish soldiers' reactions to entering or hearing about the death camps are presented on pp. 223–47.

7. See chapters 5 and 6.

8. See chapter 8. The quote is from p. 259. Moore further noted that Jewish veterans benefited from the opportunities offered by the GI Bill, including "two committed Zionists [who] chose to attend the Hebrew University in Jerusalem on the GI Bill" (pp. 260–61).

9. I use the term "American Indians" and "Native Americans" interchangeably to reflect the terminology used in current historical scholarship in the United States.

10. Statistics on Native Americans' economic, health, and educational conditions can be found in Alison R. Bernstein, *American Indians and World War II: Toward a New Era in Indian Affairs* (Norman: University of Oklahoma Press, 1991), 12–17.

11. Ibid., 19 (on voting restrictions in 1938; see pp. 138–40 on the 1948 legal cases in Arizona and New Mexico). Along with denial of voting rights, liquor prohibitions were a particular source of frustration (p. 136).

12. On the dual citizenship of Native Americans, see David E. Wilkins, *American Indian Politics and the American Political System* (Lanham, Md.: Rowman and Littlefield, 2002).

13. On Native purchase of war bonds, see Bernstein, *American Indians*, 68–70;

on home-front service, see Kenneth William Townsend, *World War II and the American Indian* (Albuquerque: University of New Mexico Press, 2000), chap. 7.

14. On draft resistance among Native groups, see Bernstein, *American Indians*, 26–28; Townsend, *World War II and the American Indian*, chap. 4. The estimate is from Bernstein, 35. On the impact of health problems and low literacy on enlistment, see Townsend, 64.

15. Bernstein explains that Collier's motives in pressing for special treatment for Indian soldiers were to preserve Indian culture and to expand the role of his agency. The head of the Navajo tribal council also asked for an indigenous regiment in order to ease the participation of Indians in the army (pp. 22–24, 40–41). The Indians' "white" identity was not universally accepted, as illustrated by instances in the South in which draft boards inducted Native Americans into segregated African American units, claiming mixed Native-Negro blood (Bernstein, *American Indians*, 41–42).

16. Bernstein described the legal battle that members of the Iroquois Confederacy, or Six Nations, fought between October 1940 and November 1941 on pp. 29–33. The case (*Ex Parte Green*) was lost on appeal in the U.S. Second Circuit Court, and the Supreme Court refused to review it. See also Townsend, *World War II and the American Indian*, 112–23. A few other Native American groups also adopted their own declarations of war (ibid., 127).

17. On the publicity that Native military participation received, much of it orchestrated by the Bureau of Indian Affairs, see Jere' Bishop Franco, *Crossing the Pond: The Native American Effort in World War II* (Denton.: University of North Texas Press, 1999), 120–48.

18. See Bernstein, *American Indians*, chap. 6. The quote is from pp. 127–28. The NCAI opposed termination without tribal consent; in 1958, tribal consent became part of a revised termination policy (pp. 173–74). A brief account of this policy shift and the political justification for it, in the context of the Native war effort, is provided by Tom Holm, "Fighting a White Man's War: The Extent and Legacy of American Indian Participation in World War II," *Journal of Ethnic Studies* 9, no. 2 (Summer 1981): 69–81. See also Townsend, *World War II and the American Indian*, chap. 8.

19. The quotes from Bernstein are on pp. 40 ("unparalleled opportunity") and 56–58.

20. Townsend, *World War II and the American Indian*. The quotes are from

pp. 138–39 ("positive attention" and "curiosity"), 184–85 (on integration in the urban workforce), and 193 ("Never before").

21. Franco, *Crossing the Pond*, 137. See pp. 87–94 on prejudices met in the workforce.

22. See "Native Sons and the Good War: Retelling the Myth of American Indian Assimilation," in *The War in American Culture: Society and Consciousness During World War II*, eds. Lewis A. Erenberg and Susan E. Hirsch (Chicago: University of Chicago Press, 1996), 217–37. The quotes are from pp. 218 ("From the official") and 221 ("In addition"). Also writing from a Native perspective, Russell Lawrence Barsh examined the impact of the warrior ideal on Native veterans in the twentieth century. Although it has deep roots in Native cultures, the warrior ideal may have hindered the veterans' ability to deal with the trauma of battle. Barsh's emphasis, like Miller's, is on the destructive impact of white wars on Native individuals and communities, not on the opportunities that they create. See "War and the Reconfiguring of American Indian Society," *Journal of American Studies* 35, no. 3 (December 2001): 371–411.

23. Bernstein, *American Indians*, 59.

24. Ibid., 133. On wartime use of Indian land by the federal government, see pp. 81–86; on the deterioration of reservation economies, see Townsend, *World War II and the American Indian*, 215–16; on the postwar drop in Indian income, both on and off reservations, see Townsend, 217–18. Native veterans encountered difficulties obtaining loans under the provisions of the GI Bill partly because of their lack of unencumbered land to be used as collateral (see Townsend, 217–18, and Bernstein, 142–43). On the economic status of urban Indians, see Bernstein, 139.

25. Christopher Paul Moore, *Fighting for America: Black Soldiers—the Unsung Heroes of World War II* (New York: Ballantine Books, 2005). The quote is from p. 51. See also Donald R. McCoy and Richard T. Ruetten, "Towards Equality: Blacks in the United States During the Second World War," in *Minorities in History*, ed. A. C. Hepburn (London: Edward Arnold, 1978), 137–42.

26. Summaries of the FEPC's limited accomplishments can be found in Adam Fairclough, *Better Day Coming: Blacks and Equality, 1890–2000* (New York: Penguin, 2001), and Thomas J. Sugrue, *Sweet Land of Liberty: The Forgotten Struggle for Civil Rights in the North* (New York: Random House, 2008).

For a specialized study, see Merl E. Reed, *Seedtime for the Modern Civil Rights Movement: The President's Committee on Fair Employment Practice, 1941–1946* (Baton Rouge: Louisiana State University Press, 1991). For a study of racial conflicts among workers at the local level, see Bruce Nelson, "Organized Labor and the Struggle for Black Equality in Mobile During World War II," *Journal of American History* 80, no. 3 (December 1993): 952–88. On civilian employment, see also McCoy and Ruetten, "Towards Equality," 142–46.

27. White protest against residential integration in Detroit's public housing (at the Sojourner Truth Homes) in February 1942 and the destructive racial confrontations that exploded in Detroit and Harlem in the summer of 1943 are examples of these tensions. See Sugrue, *Sweet Land of Liberty*, 67–70.

28. Ibid., 78–79. The black press played a key role in articulating African Americans' aspirations. For a contrasting analysis, see Lee Finkle, *Forum for Protest: The Black Press During World War II* (Rutherford, N.J.: Fairleigh Dickinson University Press, 1975) and Earnest L. Perry, Jr., "It's Time to Force a Change: The African-American Press' Campaign for a True Democracy During World War II," *Journalism History* 28, no. 2 (Summer 2002): 85–95.

29. On the relationship between black leaders and the Office of War Information (the main propaganda agency), see Clayton R. Koppes and Gregory D. Black, "Blacks, Loyalty, and Motion-Picture Propaganda in World War II," *Journal of American History* 73, no. 2 (September 1986): 383–406. See also Barbara Dianne Savage, *Broadcasting Freedom: Radio, War, and the Politics of Race, 1938–1948* (Chapel Hill: University of North Carolina Press, 1999) and Lauren Rebecca Sklaroff, "Constructing G.I. Joe Louis: Cultural Solutions to the 'Negro Problem' During World War II," *Journal of American History* 89, no. 3 (December 2002): 958–83.

30. Maureen Honey, ed., *Bitter Fruit: African American Women in World War II* (Columbia: University of Missouri Press, 1999), 16. "Heart Against the Wind," published in *The Crisis* in January 1944, is on pp. 152–55. Barnes's story, published in *Opportunity* in September 1942, is reprinted on pp. 298–303.

31. Beth Bailey and David Farber, "The 'Double-V' Campaign in World War II Hawaii: African Americans, Racial Ideology, and Federal Power," *Journal of Social History* 26, no. 4 (Summer 1993): 817–43. See also *The First Strange Place: Race and Sex in World War II Hawaii* (Baltimore: Johns Hopkins University Press, 1992), especially chap. 4.

32. Robin D. G. Kelley, *Race Rebels: Culture, Politics, and the Black Working Class* (New York: Free Press, 1994), chapter 7. Luis Alvarez, *The Power of the Zoot: Youth Culture and Resistance During World War II* (Berkeley: University of California Press, 2008), pp. 4 ("opened spaces") and 80–81 ("mobilized their bodies").

### COMMENTARY

1. For a challenging examination of these issues, see Brian Masaru Hayashi, *Democratizing the Enemy: The Japanese American Internment* (Princeton, N.J.: Princeton University Press, 2004).

### CONCLUSION

1. A good overview of the official American response to Japanese aggression in Asia can be found in Walter LaFeber, *The Clash: U.S.-Japanese Relations Throughout History* (New York: W. W. Norton, 1997). On the lobby for intervention in Asia, see Donald J. Friedman, *The Road from Isolation: The Campaign of the American Committee for Non-Participation in Japanese Aggression, 1938–1941* (Cambridge, Mass.: Harvard University Press, 1968). Waldo Heinrichs carefully traces the cautious responses to events unfolding in both Europe and Asia in *Threshold of War: Franklin D. Roosevelt and American Entry into World War II* (New York: Oxford University Press, 1988).

2. Manfred Jonas, *Isolationism in America, 1935–1941* (Ithaca, N.Y.: Cornell University Press, 1966), 23. Richard W. Steele, "The Great Debate: Roosevelt, the Media, and the Coming of the War, 1940–1941," *Journal of American History* 71, no. 1 (June 1984): 90.

3. On the racialized nature of American-Japanese relations, see John W. Dower, *War Without Mercy: Race and Power in the Pacific War* (New York: Pantheon Books, 1986). Dower does not include the pre–Pearl Harbor era in his authoritative analysis, but the lessons learned from the 1941–1945 period, paired with the recent scholarship on the debate over intervention, could yield fascinating insights.

4. Emily S. Rosenberg, *A Date Which Will Live: Pearl Harbor in American Memory* (Durham, N.C.: Duke University Press, 2003). Her fusion of "memory" and "history" in one term ("memory/history") aptly captures

the blurring of the lines—and the interaction—between public remembrance and historical interpretation that characterizes late-twentieth-century discussions of World War II, not only in America but around the world (pp. 4–5).

5. For a scholarly essay on citizenship as status, or marker of social standing, see Judith N. Shklar, *American Citizenship: The Quest for Inclusion* (Cambridge, Mass.: Harvard University Press, 1991). An insightful study that focuses on rights and obligations is Linda K. Kerber, *No Constitutional Right to Be Ladies: Women and the Obligations of Citizenship* (New York: Hill and Wang, 1998).

6. See, among others, Alice Kessler-Harris, *In Pursuit of Equity: Women, Men, and the Quest for Economic Citizenship in Twentieth-Century America* (New York: Oxford University Press, 2001).

7. The Servicemen's Readjustment Act (better known as the GI Bill) has been studied along these lines, but with a focus on how it reflected and shaped postwar, not wartime, culture.

# ACKNOWLEDGMENTS

My first acknowledgment goes to my colleague Robert D. Johnston and my publisher, Thomas LeBien, who invited me to write this short, and unconventional, volume five years ago and waited patiently for the manuscript to be completed. As was the agreement from the beginning, Thomas offered editorial advice along the way and Robert stayed at arm's length while the book was being written so as not to compromise his role as commentator. The goal we pursued was pedagogical: to present a text of undergraduate-friendly prose, with commentary, that would help students to think systematically about the choices involved in the writing of history. The arrangement worked wonderfully, as I hope the results show. I benefited tremendously from Thomas's feedback on early drafts, his timely prodding when progress was slow, and his enthusiastic support for the project throughout. I never doubted that Robert's contribution would be generous, yet searching and insightful, as I think readers will find it to be. His commitment to teaching and mentoring is exemplary.

The University of the Fraser Valley has assisted this work by providing time for writing through its Scholarly Activity, Research Option, and Sabbatical programs. I am particularly grateful to Eric Davis and Yvon Dandurand for their support. Paula Brennan and Kulwant Gill from the Interlibrary Loans office have provided essential service, and Professional Development funds have facilitated the acquisition of needed material. I have benefited from casual conversations with several colleagues, including Scott Sheffield and Chris Leach, and Bob Smith has offered reading suggestions, comments on drafts, and insights on a regular basis through the project. Barbara Messamore and Ronald Hughes lent their fine editing skills to chapter 8 prior to its publication in the *Journal of Historical Biography*. I also thank Ian Stade, special collections librarian at the Hennepin County Library, and Starr Hoffman, head of the Government Documents Department at the University of North Texas, for their assistance in obtaining reproductions of the posters used in chapter 4.

It has been a pleasure to work with Assistant Editor Daniel Crissman. He captured our goals with flair, effectively coordinated the book's various parts into a seamless whole, and smoothly guided us through the last stages of its design and production. The meticulous attention given to the manuscript by the copy editor, Emily DeHuff, is also greatly appreciated. Any interpretive, factual, or stylistic errors that may remain are mine only.

Greg Schlitt was instrumental to the project's original conceptualization, has read more than his share of chapter drafts, and, along with our children, reminds me of what most matters. For this I owe him my warmest thanks.

# INDEX

Page numbers in *italics* refer to illustrations.

# INDEX

# INDEX